Thanks for chucking that at the wall instead of me

Teaching At-Risk Children and Youth

Monica Nawrocki

Library and Archives Canada Cataloguing in Publication

Nawrocki, Monica, 1965-
        Thanks for chucking that at the wall instead of me : working with at-risk
youth / Monica Nawrocki.
    Includes bibliographical references.
    ISBN 978-1-894601-35-1
        1. Problem youth--Education. 2. Youth with social disabilities--
Education.
    I. Title.
    LC4015.N39 2005   371.93   C2005-905744-0

Cover and design by Andrea Max
Photography by Adrián Pérez
Image editor Gabriel Zelarrayan

Printed and bound in Canada.

Published by Chestnut Publishing Group
4005 Bayview Ave., Ste. 610
Toronto, ON M2M 3Z9 Canada
Tel: 416 224-5824 Fax: 416 486-4752
www.chestnutpublishing.com

We acknowledge the financial support of the Government of Canada
through the Book Publishing Industry Development Program (BPIDP)
for our publishing activities.

For Shanny . . .
who heard all these stories for the first time -
and who laughed
(and cried)
in all the right places.

Contents

PROLOGUE

When people ask me my opinion of the education system, I find it hard to know what to say. It is a system, by definition, flawed and often inadequate. However, working within it are ordinary people doing extraordinary things.

Educators are always on the verge of being overwhelmed by the constant demands of new curriculum, new technologies, new educational fads, new social trends, new government expectations, and on and on. Somehow educators manage to keep these things at bay. They are able to close the classroom door on the din of demands and create an atmosphere inside where kids feel valued, listened to, and nurtured. In my opinion, this is a minor miracle.

Every year, the challenges of the classroom are greater. Every year, more and more kids find themselves in a system that does not meet their needs. Recently, I spoke to a friend who is the secretary of a school. We talked about the fallibility of large systems and how impossible it is to meet everyone's individual needs all the time. She summed it up perfectly with these words: "It's just painful when someone doesn't fit."

This book is about kids who don't fit. Close your eyes and picture your class. Did one kid jump out of his or her seat and rudely demand your attention? That's the kid I want you to think about as you read this.

I understand what it is like to face a room of 30 demanding little beings, and know that half of your energy is going to be spent on one or two difficult kids. I know how frustrating that is.

In performing your daily minor miracle, you may never get to see a different side of that student who challenges you every day. You may never have a chance to understand where that obnoxious behaviour comes from - never know the gentle child that still resides somewhere deep inside your little classroom nemesis.

My hope is that this book may give you that chance.

Every teacher has experienced trying to explain a bad day to a non-teaching friend or partner and has seen the look of incredulity and heard remonstrations about what we should not put up with. "Well, it's not that simple ..." And we fade out, knowing the other person will not understand that while today's story might have been ugly, it is only one snapshot in a series, and it takes a long time to fill the album, make the whole story viable, and orchestrate a happy ending. It takes putting up with some stuff; it takes a lot of second, third and twelfth chances.

I just want you to know that I understand how many little faces you have in your head. I know how much of your own time you spend on paperwork. I know how seldom you can pee when you need to, how exhausted you are some nights, how you hurt when you know some of the kids suffer at home and there's nothing you can do. I know how you long for the end of the school year - and dread the goodbyes it will bring.

And I know that you may share these same feelings regardless of whether you are an educational assistant, an administrator, a coach, a social worker, a parent, a youth worker, a child care provider, a school psychologist, or a classroom teacher.

I will tell you some stories, and if laughing at me learning things the hard way will give you some food for thought, that's great. If what I found helpful in working with at-risk kids gives you an idea or two, that's wonderful. But more than anything else, as you read this book, I hope you hear me, and all the other supporters out there, whispering, "It's hard. We know. You're doing great."

Chapter One

Setting the Scene at the Centre

Talking upside down

I did not aspire to work with at-risk children. I did not streamline my education in that direction, I did not seek out employment opportunities in the field. I worked in regular classrooms for about eight years, and one day someone called me on the phone and said, "Hey, you should apply for this alternative position in our school" and presto, my life took a new direction. I applied for it because I needed a job and thought I must have a shot since they called me and encouraged me to apply. I went to a job interview at seven o'clock in the morning (NOT my optimum time), on the very last day of school in June. I was clutching a cup of coffee and contemplating the wisdom of the previous night's festivities. The hiring principal started off with a fairly benign question that sounded enormously complex to my sleep-deprived brain, so I suggested he start over and maybe ask me my name or something like that. I got the job.

I don't mean to sound flippant. Sylvia Bastable, one of the women on the hiring committee for that job, who would eventually become my boss, mentor, and friend, said she could see "the humour" from the start. My humour helped me tremendously through this professional and personal journey.

Sylvia also said that from that first meeting, she saw in me what she called a "counselling personality." During the following years we had many discussions about what exactly that meant (and how big my caseload should be as a result). Eventually I came to understand what she was getting at. She was perceptive to see anything at that early stage, though, because I was unaware of any interest or aptitude for working with difficult kids. I think what she saw was compassion. Everything else, she figured, she could teach me. She was mostly right.

So I began my journey in working with at-risk students. The job was working at a junior high school as a transition teacher with a group of seventh graders who had been identified by the sending elementary schools. The schools felt that this group of kids would have little chance of success in junior high without some intervention.

That first year was one of trial and error. Lots of both. I learned a tremendous amount, but was always frustrated with the job. What I couldn't see until much later was that I was trying to create a unique program with the same old tired building blocks I'd hauled around since university. You know the old saying, "If all you have is a hammer, everything looks like a nail." I was looking at the problems the kids were having from the wrong viewpoint. I thought I was responsible for their change. I worked my butt off and even experienced some feelings of "success" as students improved behaviourally and academically. But I nearly killed myself and I don't think many of those changes were long-term.

What I did learn that year was that kids in the classroom who look like "troublemakers" are gifted, sensitive, potential-packed little souls, often hurting, and always desperate to succeed, regardless of the fact that their actions might suggest exactly the opposite.

At the end of that eye-opening year, I had the opportunity to go to Maryland to participate in a week-long training session in Life Space Crisis Intervention. That was the turning point for me. That was when my perception shifted so that my job looked different. I left my hammer there and got some cool new tools.

Life Space Crisis Intervention (LSCI) is about talking with children and youth in crisis. The idea is that the middle of a crisis is a great learning opportunity. That in itself was a shift in thinking. I had always thought that dealing with crisis was about calming the waters as quickly as possible, figuring out who was the instigator, and administering a fair and meaningful consequence for the misbehaviour. I came to realize that with most kids, a crisis is a predictable and repetitive part of a cycle of ineffective behaviour. For young people to be able to change a pattern of behaviour into something more effective and socially acceptable, they must see that pattern. The best way to show them that pattern is for a caring adult to wade into the middle of a crisis with them.

The September after my LSCI training, I began working at the Regional Support Centre. The RSC is a small centre for students throughout the Lord Selkirk School Division in Manitoba. Typically, a student whose behaviour is becoming unmanageable in the regular classroom may be referred to the Centre. Students attend there for a minimum of eight weeks, although some remain for as long as three years. The goal is to help them identify their patterns of behaviour, make changes, and reintegrate into their home schools. This "simple" prescription can involve a myriad of different approaches, and can include numerous professionals from within or outside the school division. Rare cases may be placed in the hands of medical professionals. The Centre is a place where crisis is not feared, and where kids are viewed with compassion and treated with dignity regardless of how outrageous their behaviours might appear. It is here that my education really began.

Nothing in my university schooling prepared me for what I experienced at the RSC. The first time a student threw a binder across the classroom, yet managed to "problem solve,"[1] (deal with it, accept the consequences and end the day with a smile), I knew things were going to be different. I was on board! The first time the binder was directed towards my head and was accompanied by some choice names for me, I was far less on board. It took a while, but eventually I could be just as happy about a positive resolution when I was the target of the aggression. I guess that was the first big lesson of the RSC: you can't take it personally. That binder and all the others that followed it were not about me, and if I hadn't gotten past the "righteous indignation," I would have missed out on everything.

My stories are all set at the RSC, and the lessons I learned came from there, so I want to paint a quick picture before we continue.

The year I joined the staff at the RSC, there was one classroom with a teacher/counsellor and a teacher assistant (TA), plus a director, who was also a teacher and counsellor. Seven years later there was a director, three classrooms, each with a teacher and full-time TA, and varying numbers of other TAs depending on funding for individual students. For example, a student whose needs were severe enough to qualify them for Level 3 funding would have a full-time TA. As a result, the group of three I joined in 1995 was a team of eight to ten (depending on the clientele) in 2002 when I left. Class sizes ranged from six to ten pupils on average. The two directors of the Centre, first Sylvia Bastable and then her partner, Bob Bastable, both created and continue to encourage a team approach to dealing with students. All staff deal with all students, and staff consult together weekly to discuss students, progress and strategies. Less formal debriefing and consulting happen constantly.

In addition to the three classrooms, the Centre has a common area with a ping pong table and couches, a kitchen where everyone eats lunch together, an office, bathrooms, a meeting room, and a Quiet Room. The Quiet Room is in the elementary classroom and is available for students to take a timeout of their own choosing, one suggested by a peer or adult, or one chosen and enforced by an adult. The students are welcome in all rooms at appropriate times and are remarkably respectful of these boundaries.

Kids at the Centre quickly learn that problem-solving is a requirement. They learn that their behaviour will draw very different reactions, or lack of reactions, from the adults here, as compared to those at their home school or their home. They learn that there are very few non-negotiables and that whatever happens, they will eventually have to talk about it. Not hear about it - talk about it. No one requires eye contact and "sitting up at the table." Kids talk from the floor, from behind the couch, while sitting on their heads, through puppets, with fake voices, in the car, through notes, while drawing, on the swings, through locked doors, and on the phone. But they talk.

The result of talking: being heard. That is one of the main things that is different for kids at the Centre. With the luxury of time not afforded to our counterparts in the regular system, teachers at the Centre can usually take the time or make the time to listen. The feedback from students confirms that this simple concept has a powerful impact and the knowledge that they will be heard is a necessary part of the change process.

One fruit of listening is understanding. To hear a student explain an event, with a few questions here and there, is to gain insight into the motivation behind the behaviour.

The Centre, with its intimate setting and family-like feeling, is where I got my education as a teacher. Let me tell you a story or two ...

1. Problem-solving is the term used to describe the process of working through a crisis with a student. The stages include helping the young person to "de-escalate" and become calm and relaxed enough to discuss the incident, identifying the facts and chronology of the incident, exploring the student's role, and hopefully, learning about behaviour patterns and positive strategies for change. (Long & Wood, Life Space Intervention: Talking With Children and Youth in Crisis, 1991)

Chapter Two

Positive Reinforcement

Thanks for chucking that at the wall instead of me

I am sitting at my desk near the end of my first day with my new class. There are only six students. It's a large, bright classroom. I have lots of resources, a great teacher assistant, and supportive colleagues. It is the perfect teaching situation. It should be the perfect teaching situation.

My pencil is poised over the Caught Book; a notebook in which I have decided to make a note every time I catch one of the kids being good. My pencil has been poised here several times today, yet the page remains blank. I look around the room: one student is sitting at his desk, carving his initials into the wood and staring at me defiantly, eagerly anticipating a challenge. Another is quietly ripping up all the work he completed today. Two others are calling each other names I have never even heard before. One is standing at the door demanding to be dismissed. The last has locked himself in the bathroom and is refusing to come out. Their coats and backpacks are strewn around the room, save one jacket hanging on the coat rack. Papers, books and art supplies are everywhere. Sighing wearily, I put down my pencil, choose a crisis, and go deal with it.

At the end of that day, after we'd talked about swearing, name-calling, wood-carving, work-ripping and dismissal times, we gathered at the table for Group. I looked around at all the grumpy little faces and wondered if we were going to get through this day without more drama. I handed out the daily report cards and watched with amazement as each boy in turn read his score, and realized that, despite the end-of-the-day crisis period, he'd had a pretty good day. I saw shoulders straighten, I saw eyes which had been avoiding mine, look at me. I even saw smiles. I watched them respond to the positive comments I'd written on their reports like sunflowers turning to face the sun.

I decided that the next day I would do a better job of the Caught Book because I could see that those positive messages were going to be huge! I read my sole entry from the Caught Book for day one: Darren, thanks for hanging up your jacket when you came in this morning. The next morning, every one of them hung up their jackets!

From the start, the Caught Book became an integral part of our program. The kids were adamant that we read from the book EVERY day, regardless of what was going on. Even if we had been on a field trip all day without the book, they would insist we read it. So I would pretend to read and make up little nuggets for them about things I had noticed and appreciated during the day. They knew I wasn't really reading but they didn't care. They loved hearing anything that was positive and specifically about them.

This may be the most profound lesson of my years at the RSC: you can't build anything on a foundation of failure. Until kids experience the feeling of success, they simply cannot buy into anything you are trying to generate. They will remain stuck in an ongoing cycle of self-defeating behaviour if all they hear is what they are doing wrong. I tried not to nag or even ask, but just to be vigilant until I caught someone doing what I hoped to see and then thanked them for it. This was my main strategy for creating routines in the classroom. I involved the kids in creating some expectations for behaviour. I laid them out very, very clearly and specifically. Then I lurked around waiting for someone to accidentally adhere to the rules, and wham! - I'd nail them in the Caught Book and they'd start doing it regularly!

When we had an especially rude group, we focused on catching them saying "please" or "thank you" and targeted manners. Improving our manners became a game and soon they were practising formal introductions with any unsuspecting visitor who came into the classroom. After a while, it became a less frequent topic in the Caught Book, reappearing only when staff noticed a return to cruder ways and a tune-up was required.

With a messy group, the Caught Book focused on the kids taking care of their area and their property. With a group that didn't get along well, we focused on positive interactions between them and anything we could call "respectful" behaviour towards one another. With a group with especially bad social skills, we targeted positive friendship skills.

Obviously, this one technique was used in harmony with many others. For every comment on good friendship skills, there may have been several problem-solving sessions, a group discussion, a formal lesson and a role play or two. But the idea of the Caught Book is what is important, not the book itself. By creating a tangible practice, staff reminded ourselves constantly that we needed to be positive with the kids as much as possible. I read somewhere that if a person is going to truly hear you when you bring a criticism to his or her attention, you must have pointed out seven previous positives. That ratio is quite a challenge, but the point is that positive reinforcement works. It doesn't matter how you do it. At the RSC, oral positive feedback was given at every opportunity from all staff to all students. Our classroom had its Caught Book, others had their own routines, and all three classrooms used a daily report card, completed and discussed at noon and the end of the day. Kids have to know what they are doing right. When kids have experienced some taste of success and start to believe in themselves the slightest bit, they develop the courage they need to really look at themselves and start to make changes in their behaviour.

I had many students tell me that they were stupid. I asked one boy how he knew that, and he looked at me with exasperation and explained that his dad and brother told him so. I could have told that little guy every day that he was not stupid and it would have been meaningless. When I pointed out specific examples of how quickly he figured out a puzzle or caught on to a new concept in math or learned the rules to a new game in gym, he had to admit that the evidence was starting to suggest something new. I wasn't placating him; I was drawing his attention to facts and letting him draw his own conclusions.

Many of them also believed that they were bad. I talked with one little boy who told me he was bad and that the devil was in him. He raised his pant leg, placed his hand halfway up his calf and told me, "I'm only good up to about here. The rest is bad."

Another boy was a wonderful artist. I thought I'd found an instant "in." I complimented a picture he had drawn, and he immediately ripped it up and threw it away. Remarkably, it took three destroyed masterpieces for me to figure out he was ripping them up because of my compliments. We started very slowly with him, commenting on things less personal to him, slowly building his comfort with accepting compliments. I told him it was hard for me to accept compliments and asked if he would help me work on that. We'd sit in the Quiet Room making up outrageous compliments to pay one another and then giggling about them. A lot of them involved the quality of farts and burps. What can I say? He was eleven.

In time, he stopped participating in group from behind the couch and sat with us, without looking up or speaking. One day, he was able to accept a compliment about the quality of his math homework. After many months he let us put his art on the wall.

Surprising kids with positive reinforcement is also very valuable. In some ways, I feel that this is the best method. It is not predictable, is not in danger of becoming routine and losing meaning. And the kids can't expect or demand it. For example, if you use a method of reinforcement or reward that gives students a five-minute free-time coupon for every half hour of math they do, they may soon be manipulating the situation. "Well I did 15 minutes of math before I threw the chair. Where's my two and a half minutes of free time?"

With the right student, these "deals" work well to get them going. Sometimes, they are the only way to get the ball rolling. We have had students come to the Centre who have refused to do any work in a certain subject. They managed to stick to it long enough to be removed from class, and eventually their school, by engaging the adults in a colossal power struggle. For a kid like that, very different work and a tangible, achievable reward are definitely appropriate tools. The goal is to move on, lessen fear, develop comfort and skills. To make extrinsic motivation become intrinsic. Intermittent reward is great for helping kids move through those stages.

Often I would stop the class when they were all working quietly, thank them and tell them why I thought that silent work time was so important. Then I would tell them we were having an unscheduled fun activity as a reward.

If an individual in the class was struggling with some assignment, its completion might result in a celebratory dip into the treat bag for everyone in the class. Rewarding the whole group for an individual accomplishment was used intermittently. It fostered the group cohesiveness we worked so hard to create, and the byproduct was that they often gave each other specific encouragement and positive support. Having students copy our positive messages was a very powerful tool. For a student to hear from a peer that he or she did a good job on a science assignment was far more valuable than hearing it from an adult.

One Friday, with a group of kids between the ages of eight and 11 who got along unusually well, I invited everyone to stop working five minutes early and go for a little extra recess to celebrate the fact that Kevin had brought a good lunch and eaten it every day that week. (That was a HUGE accomplishment.) They all slapped Kevin on the back as they roared out of the room to play ping pong. When we had reconvened in the classroom 20 minutes later, the youngest member of the group came up and whispered in my ear, "Kevin had a healthy snack during the break. Should we have another recess?"

The daily report cards were the baseline of the program. The report cards had many categories to evaluate and beside each one, a score of 1, 2, or 3 could be awarded. No zeros!

The categories ranged from being at school to the quality of academic work. There were areas for social skills, behaviour expectations and academic goals. For kids who have experienced nothing but failure and criticism on report cards, it is a very big thing to receive a positive daily report with a high score. A student's first few days were usually pretty good - we called it the Honeymoon Period. Many kids achieved a perfect score on their first day. Most of them looked as if we had just promoted them to the next grade. I can recall many tough young teenagers slouching casually around the Centre at the end of the day, pretending to be bored, and making sure every staff member from every classroom had seen their report card before they left.

The report card gave us an objective medium through which to target inappropriate behaviour. It also helped maintain relationships because the students earned their score; it was not subjective. When you give someone the finger, you lose a point for "Verbal/Nonverbal Communication." I don't dislike you; that's just how it is.

I'm not suggesting that I never had a report card thrown in my face, but it was palatable to say, "Oh, bummer, your report card was below your target score this morning. No break this afternoon. Want me to sit at your desk with you?" Far better than, "I don't like your behaviour. You sit at your desk." The report card became the bad guy so the adults could remain the coaches, supporters, and friends.

The report card was useful in correcting behaviour in a more immediate sense. If students were out of their desk, wandering about the room, I could simply remind them quietly that they might be affecting their report card score for "Remaining in Assigned Area." The decision was theirs, of course.

The report card also helped both the student and the staff member to see the day as a whole. When a student ended his day by throwing a bowl of spaghetti leftovers at the TA, it could be difficult to remember that the rest of his day might have been excellent. The report card, half of it having been completed at noon, had already recorded an excellent morning, so no matter how cheesed off the adults may have been about the spaghetti, one ugly incident could not nullify the hard work of the rest of the day. The student did not have to go home thinking about the one incident in the day that would reinforce negative beliefs about self.

This is more important with some kids than others. I can think of one in particular who was very hard on himself. When he began to struggle, he got so tense his behaviour worsened automatically. As we tried to gently help him stay on course, he perceived help as correction, decided he was "in trouble" and panicked. We would try to avoid anything he could perceive as correction or "being in trouble." Inevitably, he would decide he had ruined his day, give up, and all hell would break loose. We had a lot of those days before the constant positive messages began to touch him. One teacher assistant in particular who worked with him in his home school before and after his time at the RSC, understood his pattern perfectly and did a good job of giving him positive feedback, disguising her guidance of his behaviour as his own idea, and being very present with him when he had to deal with consequences. His slow acceptance that he might be a "good kid" made a difference. We are what we believe we are.

I think it was watching this student in particular that got me thinking about how hard I was on myself sometimes. As I reminded him and the other students that we would celebrate mistakes because they helped us learn, I was wondering why I had such difficulty forgiving myself at times. I took a tentative step toward being a little gentler with myself.

With children who showed outrageous behaviour, it could be extremely difficult to find positives. Once the honeymoon was over, many kids slid right to the bottom of their patterns of ineffective behaviour. During the first weeks of a student's time at the Centre, it is not unusual to find yourself saying things like, "Thanks for chucking that at the wall instead of me." That may seem crazy. But what if the child is truly out of control? What if he is filled with the rage of abandonment or abuse? What if every single day that he has come to school, he has lost it and hurt someone? What if he has been suspended or expelled more than he's been in school, and now has the anger of academic delays and failures to add to the mix? And what if the buck stops with you? You can't send him home. You might be his last hope. You could probably say very sincerely when he hesitated before beaning you, and then changed his mind, "Thanks for chucking that at the wall instead of me."

I think of one student, a 13-year-old boy with just such a rage. He did a fair bit of damage to the building during a stressful time. One day, I had to call his dad about something. It wasn't anything major, but Pete was upset. He glared at me in a rage as I dialed, punched a hole the size of a grapefruit through the wall of the classroom, and ran out of the Centre. When I went to sit with him on the swings where he had run, he was sobbing. As usual, he expressed a great deal of regret for his actions and total frustration at his feeling of being unable to control his temper. I waited until I was sure he could hear me and then I told him clearly that I believed he did feel out of control and that he didn't mean to break the wall. I told him that I felt he had more control than he thought because he had not hurt anyone. I reminded him of his previous school where he had hurt many people and pointed out that he had not touched anyone during his weeks at the Centre. He stopped crying, and I could tell he was listening as he had never listened to me before. I pointed out to him that he had chosen to hit a wall instead of me and that showed compassion - a great quality. (He squirmed a little when I used the word "chosen" but did not argue.)

I reminded him that he would be able to fix the hole in the wall or pay to have it fixed, but if he had chosen to hurt someone, there would be nothing he could do to take that action back. He sat quietly for a long time and then confessed that he always tried hard not to get mad. He tried really, really hard not to hit people, but if he did, he figured they hated him anyway and then he didn't try very hard anymore.

He told me a lot of other things that day at the swings. Many of them were key in helping us understand Pete and in setting up a system to help him to cope with his aggression. I believe going out there with punishment on the brain might have felt good for me. I hate "hole-y" walls! However, I would never have gotten his attention the way I did, would never have gained that bit of trust, would never have learned so much from him sharing his heart at that moment of vulnerability, if I hadn't found something positive to say.

Pete's story is not unique. Students who came to us in a spiral of aggressive behaviour, had often not heard an encouraging word in a long time. They seemed trapped in a cycle of self-hatred that was manifested in "bad behaviour," which brought them reactions from adults to confirm their notions of themselves and fuel the self-hatred. It is hard to act good when you don't feel good. We felt our first job at the Centre was to make failure as difficult as possible.

All students are asked to set goals for themselves when they begin at the Centre. Every day that they meet their own goals, they earn a checkmark. "Goal Activity" brings a special event or trip to reward all students with enough checkmarks. At entry level, you'd pretty much need to torch the building to miss Goal Activity (a successful torching, not just an attempt, as happened with the boy who set the toilet paper roll on fire on his first day).

In my classroom, the adults set goals too. Real goals: smoke less, stop swearing, swim three times a week, drink less coffee. Mine were usually to swim regularly before school, to drink less coffee, and to handle my stress appropriately in the classroom. Some groups were more vigilant than others about checking up on the adults. The obsessive-compulsive kids were great for keeping you in line. I had a kid ask me every day for a year whether I had gone swimming that morning or not. "No, I didn't. Thanks for asking."

We encouraged the kids to set attainable goals like "getting to school on time," or "trying all work." We also encouraged them to set ones we could manipulate a little to "help" them get to Goal Activity when they needed it. "Getting along with others" was my favourite because it was pretty hard to go an entire day without having a single positive interaction with anyone. Not impossible, mind you, but pretty hard. "Well, I think you should get your check for today. Remember when the janitor came in this morning and you said hello?"

The point here is that it was important to create success right away when a student first arrived. The typical reaction of at-risk kids when they hear about Goal Activity is: "I won't be going. I haven't been allowed on a field trip since kindergarten." The typical reaction of RSC kids when the first Goal Activity rolls around and they find out they have enough checks to go: "Holy shit!"

I once heard the story of how whales are trained. Apparently a rope is laid across the bottom of the whale's tank. Every time the whale swims over it, it receives a reward. The rope is raised off the bottom of the tank, not high enough for the whale to go beneath it. Again, every time it swims over the rope, the whale gets a treat. Eventually, the rope is raised high enough that the whale can go over or under. Every time the whale goes over, it gets a reward. Every time it goes under, it gets a scolding. Just kidding. Nothing happens. It can go over or under, but if it goes over, it gets a reward. Higher and higher the rope goes until it is at the surface of the pool and then, out of the pool. Eventually, you can get a two-ton whale to jump over a rope.

Think about your most challenging student. Lay the rope on the bottom of the pool and start over.

Chapter Three

Problem Solving

What were you thinking?

L et me tell you about Dale, a nine-year-old with poor impulse control. He loved ping pong, and it was a source of constant irritation to him that there were other students at the Centre because it meant he had to share the table, wait his turn and all those annoying things. We had been coaching Dale on his social skills and giving him specific ways to work on making friends. One day, I stopped Dale on his way out for break and reminded him to think about his actions and try to do something that might build a friendship that recess. I should have been more specific.

Moments later I heard yelling and running footsteps and went out to see Dale running at top speed with two of the boys from the older class chasing him. Dale had the ping pong ball in his hand and, unfortunately for his well-being, was refusing to let go of it. The boys got to him a step ahead of me. We talked while Dale held an ice pack on his face. I had gotten the facts from the incensed older boys: they were in the middle of an important game (part of the Centre tournament play), when Dale grabbed the ball in mid-air and started running.

I resisted the familiar urge to ask Dale, "What were you thinking?"

He had been at the Centre for a couple of months already and so it was he who suggested, from beneath his ice pack, "I think we need to problem-solve."

"Problem solving" is a term borrowed from Life Space Crisis Intervention. At the Centre, it became our term for talking. Many of our kids came to us with negative mindsets about talking. When we used the word "talk," most kids heard "lecture," or "scold," or "trouble." When we said it was time to "problem-solve," the response was different. They soon learned this meant that they would get to tell their side of the story and it would be listened to without judgment. They also learned that they had a pretty good shot at resolving the problem. Older students resisted more and so, as much as possible, we gave the kids latitude in controlling the when and where of problem-solving. The little ones, with fewer defenses and "baggage," were often pushing us to "pwoblem-tholve."

I will not attempt to explain the ideas of Dr. Long and Dr. Wood. I wholeheartedly recommend that you learn about Life Space Crisis Intervention for yourself. What I will do is tell you what LSCI means for me.

One of the things I lacked that first year of working with at-risk kids at the junior high school was an idea of who I needed to be during a student's crisis. I assumed my job was that of moral thermometer. I felt the kids often lacked clear ideas about right and wrong and I can remember listening to kids tell me stories while I reminded myself to look disapproving. I actually distracted myself from being a good listener, because I thought it was my job to frown or cluck my tongue when the story got to the part about sneaking out the bedroom window or slashing a tire or running away from the police. I thought the kids would interpret a neutral face as condoning their behaviour. How I wish I could have another shot at that year!

LSCI changed that completely. It requires that I be present with kids when they are upset, help them be calm enough to talk, and listen to their story with no judgment. That is the first phase. After that, I will use questions and clarification to determine the details of the events as clearly as possible. Last, I will determine what the situation calls for, choose a direction to move in, and assist the students to see the meaning behind their actions. Hopefully, the result is learning for the students, about their patterns of behaviour, about how those patterns negatively affect their lives, about how they can work to change them. Sometimes, it takes a lot of problem solving just to help a student see the pattern and then a whole lot more to begin to address it. The point is, LSCI provides a framework to use and a role for the adult to play. Knowing my role in dealing with kids was something more like counsellor, coach, or friend, was far more appealing to me than Dispenser of Justice. When I began to use LSCI, I was amazed to find that once kids had worked through a problem with me and had even been able to see their contribution to the problem, they were far more willing to discuss consequences.

Let me demonstrate what I mean by sharing the problem-solving session with Dale and his ice pack.

So, there I was, staring at him with exasperation, thinking, "What the heck were you thinking?" I spent some time ensuring his injuries were not serious but consoling him about them anyway. Without interrupting, I let him vent about the boys who tackled him. I asked if he was ready to talk about it a bit and he agreed.

I asked how his evening the previous night had been, what he had for supper, whether his parents were home, if he got a good sleep. I asked about breakfast, the mood at home in the morning, the bus ride to school and his first hour of school. The reason for the "backtracking" is that a huge percentage of the incidents we dealt with at the Centre were surface incidents resulting from heightened emotions about a deeper issue. Often the more significant incident originated at home, and when kids are emotionally flooded just after or during a crisis, they are very likely to let you know, consciously or unconsciously, where the real issue is hiding. Those few simple questions were often enough to find our way into stories that were a long way from the argument or incident at hand. Dale's situation was not about any outside problem, so there was nothing of note in the "backtracking" information.

Our problem-solving session went something like this:

Monica: Well, Dale, I saw the boys tackle you and I saw you not hit back - good job! That's about all I did see. Why don't you tell me what happened, and maybe start right from when you left the classroom for break.

Dale: I wanted to play ping pong so I grabbed the ball. They got all mad and started chasing me and Keith punched me and . . .

(I let him vent again about the "whuppin'" he took.)

Monica: So, you went out of the classroom, straight over to the table and grabbed the ball. Did you say anything?

D: I think I said I wanted to play.

M: Did anyone else say anything?

D: No, they just started chasing me!

M: Did you notice what was going on when you grabbed the ball?

D: Huh?

(Not a great question, as Dale pointed out so eloquently.)

M: Where was Keith standing?

D: At one end of the ping pong table.

M: Where was Brian?

D: At the other end.

M: Mmm. I wonder what they were doing before you got there?

D: They were having a game, I guess. (Small flicker of light bulb.)

M: Can you remember what you thought just before you grabbed the ball?

D: I thought that I wanted to play.

M: Why did you want to play?

D: (With disgust.) Because I love ping pong. Duh!

M: Yeah, I know you love it and you're getting pretty good, aren't you?

D: Yeah. The older guys will play with me sometimes now.

M: So you're making friends by playing ping pong? Wow, that's great.

D: You told me to go make a friend, you know. And then I end up gettin' punched by that ... (a little more venting).

M: Hang on, Dale. I want to make sure I understand what you're saying. You said that I told you to "go make a friend." Is that right?

D: Yeah.

M: You sound a little mad when you say that. Why?

D: Because you told me to make a friend and I tried and look what happened!

M: You were trying to make friends with Keith and Brian?

D: Yes!

M: Well, that's a good thing. It's really good to want to make friends. What was your plan?

D: To play ping pong with them and be their friend.

M: Oh. I think I get it now. You know I'm old, Dale, so help me through this one more time, okay? You heard what I said about trying out a friendship skill. You decided that playing ping pong with the guys would be the way to go. Is that right so far?

D: Yeah.

M: So you are going to try to make some friends, which is a really good thing, you decide to do that by playing ping pong with them, which is a good idea. And then you leave the classroom and what happens?

D: I grabbed the ball so they'd have to let me play.

M: I see. So now that you can look back at the whole thing, how good a plan was that?

D: It sucked.

M: Well, it started out really well but it didn't end up the way you wanted, did it?

D: No.

M: I think we're really starting to get somewhere, here. Are you okay to stay and chat a little more? You're doing some really awesome problem-solving here.

D: Okay.

M: Are you interested in looking at your plan to see if we could improve it in case you ever want to try again?

D: I am not going to try again.

M: Okay. But maybe one of the other kids might want some advice about friendship skills. Or maybe you might change your mind some day. What do you think?

D: Whatever.

M: So let's look at that plan again. Let's draw it on a map. Here's you with an idea.

D: Is that supposed to be a light bulb?

M: Give me a break, would ya? So here you are with a great idea to make friends by playing ping pong. What came next?

D: I went to the ping pong table, and . . .

M: Hold on. I'm going to put you at the ping pong table. How is it so far? The plan, not my drawing!

D: (giggling) Okay so far.

M: What's next?

D: I grab the ball.

M: Right. Next?

D: They start chasing me.

M: Okay. Can you see where your plan got off course yet?

D: Yup. When I grabbed the ball.

M: I think you're right. I wonder why that didn't work?

D: I think it was because they were in the middle of a game. If someone did that to me, I'd be mad. But I wouldn't pound them!

M: Really? What would you do?

D: I'd let them play!

M: (skeptically) Really?

D: No. Maybe I'd tell them, "Hey, if you give the ball back, I'll have you the next game."

M: Wow! Great idea. Maybe we'll suggest that to Keith and Brian when we problem-solve with them, eh? And I bet they would like to know why you took the ball. I wonder what they think about that now.

D: They probably think I was just trying to piss them off.

M: Probably. We'll be able to talk about that too. (We made a specific plan about what to cover when we problem-solved with the other two boys.)

D: What about my report card?

M: What do you think?

D: I'm probably going to lose a point for "Getting along with peers," right?

M: Yup.

D: Are you going to call my dad?

M: Well, I have to call and explain the bruise, don't I? If anyone is going to be in trouble, it will probably be me, because you got hurt at school. I'm sorry about that, Dale. Don't worry. I'm pretty excited to tell your dad about how you didn't hit back and how amazing you were in problem solving. Why don't you help me write out what I'll say so I get it right?

D: Okay. Maybe if those guys say sorry for hitting me, I'll say sorry for grabbing the ball.

M: Cool! Thanks for all this hard work, Dale. Shall we go do some work in the classroom or do you want to talk to the guys right away?

D: I'll talk to them later.

M: OK. I'll go set up a meeting for right before lunchtime. You can head back to the classroom. Could you tell Terry to give you three points on your report card for problem solving? Thanks.

I could hear him happily yelling to Terry about his points for problem solving well before he hit the classroom!

If that sounded a bit like a transcript from the television program, "Columbo," there is a reason. When I took LSCI training, Dr. Long used that exact analogy when discussing the importance of asking lots of questions and clarifying things. Often, that is all that is required. Many kids pick up on what went wrong as soon as you spread the picture out in front of them. They will often see immediately where they got off track, when you establish a clear and full reconstruction of the sequence of events or "Timeline."[2]

You may also have noticed a lot of positive reinforcement along the way. This is critical to keep the kids engaged in the process. It also builds rapport, and their confidence.

In Dale's case, he needed a little more help than just the timeline, and once we had that established, I decided that he needed some New Tools.[3] This is one of the LSCI interventions. It is used in scenarios where a kid has the right motivation but his methodology is all messed up. This is one that I used a lot. Over seven years at the Centre, I learned that most of the time, when you find yourself musing, "What were you thinking?" a little investigation will uncover the answer. And it won't be nearly as crazy as you think.

Take John, for example. He was being transitioned back to his school after his time at the Centre. He went part-time to his home school and part-time to the RSC. This allowed us to problem-solve at the Centre any incidents that could not be addressed at the school. One day, we received a call from John's principal to inform us that John had been sent home and was in some major doo-doo. (Those may not have been his exact words.)

It seems that John was not cutting it in the classroom - out of his desk, talking, off-task, etc. After many unsuccessful reminders in the room, the teacher asked him to step out into the hall, presumably to give him a little tune-up. John flatly refused to leave the room. In response to his defiance, she asked him to go to the office and wait for her there. Again, John refused. She then ordered him to the office and again he refused. It ended with the teacher feeling forced to call the office to have someone come and remove John from the classroom.

"What was he thinking?" the Centre staff asked each other in exasperation. The director, Sylvia, did the problem-solving with John the next day. Guess what? John had a clear plan. He had been told by his grandmother that if he got kicked out of class at his home school, he was going to be in big trouble at home. John tried hard to be good in class, but his hyperactivity got the best of him. When he realized he was in trouble, he remembered his grandmother's warning and decided he must not leave the room at any cost so he wouldn't be in trouble with her. The further down the road he got, the more aware he became that he might be making it worse, but he was panicked and without many resources for making a new plan on the spot. So he stuck to his guns and went down in flames!

Another case, this one from my year in the Transition program at the junior high school: I was called to a classroom to "retrieve" one of my Grade 7 students the first week of school. When I arrived, Jason was standing on his desk, yelling obscenities. I coaxed him off the desk and out of the room and took him to a quiet spot. I immediately asked him, "What were you thinking?" (I hadn't taken LSCI yet!)

With very sloppy skills, I managed to recreate the scenario with Jason. It ended up going back to a wild morning at home that caused him to miss the bus and be dropped off at school just as the bell was ringing. He got to his locker as his classmates were heading down the hall to their first class. Here is the crux of the problem: Jason had not yet mastered how to use his combination lock or to read his timetable. Grade 7 was a whole new ball game with rotating classes and a timetable and several teachers and lockers with touchy combination locks. Most grade 7 students are completely confused for most of September. (Do NOT get me started on this system!)

By the time he got his locker open (after several tries), he looked at his incomprehensible timetable, grabbed a couple of books at random, saw the last kid from his class rounding the corner of the hall, and followed him to class. Jason found himself in math class with a social studies textbook. When the math teacher finished his lesson and asked them to open their texts, Jason got a little anxious. When the teacher started going over the questions orally, Jason responded to his heightening anxiety by distracting himself with a little conversation with his neighbour. When the teacher called on him to answer one of the questions in the book, Jason made a snap decision, probably not even consciously. He decided if he was going to be singled out and embarrassed in front of his new classmates, he was not going to be made to look stupid. Any kid will choose to look bad over stupid. So Jason made some sarcastic remark that was definitely not the answer to the math question. The teacher responded negatively and they were off.

By the time I got there, the situation had escalated to Jason standing on his desk, reciting all the swear words he could think of at the top of his lungs. No one in that room noticed that he had the wrong textbook and no one knew he couldn't read a timetable.

If I had a nickel for every time some outrageous behaviour could be traced back to some simple little thing like that, I'd be rich. Most kids just handle those little glitches. They admit they have the wrong text and share with another student. They ask for help with their locker or with reading a timetable. They have the skills to address minor problems and solve them alone. But the kids we are talking about simply don't have those resources. Without problem solving, Jason would have been punished for his behaviour, missed class, gotten further behind, and still not known how to read his timetable. That is how a cycle continues.

Once we had addressed the real problems that were bothering him, he accepted the consequences for his behaviour. All too often, we punish a behaviour that is a side issue for students. They don't feel heard, or helped, and, as Sylvia used to say, the real issue is buried, but definitely not dead.

I found LSCI was my most valuable tool during my years at the Centre. I believe it is a truly timeless technique that really works, with almost any person or problem. I also think it was effective because it was used by everyone at the Centre. It was THE tool. We all had our own styles, of course, but because it was so universal, the kids knew what to expect, they began to believe in the process and less energy was used up in getting the kids to talk. They were, for the most part, not resistant to problem solving. Also, because it was presented as a skill that everyone at the RSC was required to learn, and because the adults were all vigilant about praising the kids for their problem-solving skills, it could often become a matter of pride for kids. I remember many times, getting a young person to problem solve by asking him or her to "help" a newer student.

I recall the first time Ralph volunteered to problem solve: he was 14, very tough and had been resistant to everything, including problem solving. One day, Ralph was involved with a new student in a minor altercation that Ralph had not initiated. This was a first. I watched as Ralph slowly realized that he was "kinda the good guy" on this one. He knew he would be required to talk about what had happened, regardless of his role. He looked at the other kid, at the adult who had intervened, cleared his throat and said, "I can show that kid how to problem solve if you want."

Many times, we used the peer-helper approach to engage kids in the process and to develop their skills. Students often took visible pride in their problem-solving skills and were anxious to show them off to their home-school teachers. We often heard the kids telling their visiting teachers that they had learned how to problem solve. And, because problem solving gave us a tool with which to help kids understand and change behaviour, we soon heard the same kids reporting things like, "I've learned how to control my anger," or, "I do math now." or "I'm finally learning to read."

Personally, I doubt I could have worked with the kids at the Centre without training in LSCI. As I said earlier, I didn't have any special training to work with at-risk kids. With no specific skills, an average teacher (that's me) was soon able to help kids who would have scared me silly earlier in my career. I never felt lost, because I always had a plan to follow. I often ended up at a dead end and had to ask for help from talented superiors, but I was rarely afraid to jump into a crisis because I knew precisely how to start. Most importantly, I believed in the process. There might not be learning and insight in every problem-solving session, but there were always positive outcomes. I remember looking at my boss in exasperation one day as the student we had been problem solving with suddenly jumped up and stormed out of the room. I thought it had been going so well! "It's all just information," Bob said. He and I went back over the whole session and thought about where in the conversation the student showed signs of agitation and the topic we were on right when the student stormed out. We realized we had just stumbled onto an issue of which we had been previously unaware.

There is still merit in a session that ended poorly or one that did not appear to provide any insight to the student or the adult. For kids who don't trust adults, going through problem solving is a huge experience: an adult is willing to be with them even when they are upset. The adult is not telling them what to do, but asking them what is wrong. They are listened to, comforted, soothed. They are treated with respect and their problems and their feelings are taken seriously. Some kids blossom within this process. They understand it quickly, participate willingly, pay attention to what they are learning. Other students may never see the process as anything but "what you have to do to get back in class." Either way, change comes and it is a wonderful thing to witness.

2. Timeline is the term we used at the RSC for step #2 in the LSI strategy. Referred to there as Students in Crisis Need to Talk, this step requires the helping adult to ask clarifying questions to expand the story from the student. The purpose of step 2 is to give the students the opportunity to tell their story and to give the adult a clear picture of what occurred and how the students in question played a role. (Long & Wood, Life Space Intervention: Talking With Children and Youth in Crisis, 1991)

3. New Tools is one of the five main types of interviews a helping adult can choose to use in LSI. This particular approach would be used with a student who has the right idea and positive motivation, but uses inappropriate methods to pursue goals. (Long & Wood, 1991)

Chapter 4

Avoiding Conflict

Let's make a deal

How do you know when you are mishandling a conflict? What are the subtle clues, the gentle nuances? One day at the Centre I could not get into my classroom because a ten-year-old had barricaded the door with furniture. As he screamed at me from the other side of the door, I sensed I might not have handled that conflict quite as well as I could have.

We have all had incidents in which we have ended up in a power struggle with a kid. It may have started slowly, but at the end we are looking around in amazement, thinking, "How did I get here?" This does not mean we are bad people; it just means we're people.

Conflict is a funny thing. As soon as we hear the word, most of us are a little uncomfortable. We tend to view conflict as negative and almost all of us will avoid it if possible. In reality, conflict is a part of everyday life, unavoidable. The outcome and even the process can be a negative experience, but conflict itself is neutral. Conflict simply means that something has come between me and my goal. I have decided to get a cup of coffee from the coffee machine, and a colleague has stopped me en route to ask a question. Few of us will struggle with this conflict or even feel negatively about it (unless it's the day's first cup of coffee, of course). I handle the obstruction; perhaps even see the positive outcome of having taken care of my colleague's question, and carry on to my cup of coffee.

But what if I was heading for the boss's office with a finished report? Perhaps the colleague's interruption was a request that would force me to rewrite the report in my hand (the one I stayed up half the night to finish). Now I may see this situation as a conflict. Ironically, my colleague may not see this as a conflict at all.

That's another thing about conflict: everyone defines it differently.

I have asked groups of people to define conflict and have received answers ranging from "disagreement" to "fist fight." Our families of origin have a lot to do with how we define it. In my family, hesitating to agree was a conflict! Imagine my discomfort once at a friend's home when there was a heated debate over a political issue. They were yelling at each other to make their points. My mind was screaming, "Conflict! Conflict! Duck and cover!" When I got my heart rate under control, and the blood stopped rushing in my ears enough for me to hear, they were happily clearing the table for dessert and commenting on the "great debate."

When we feel we are faced with conflict, we experience immediate physiological and psychological responses. Most of us, if the conflict appears serious enough, will experience our anthropologically inherited response: fight or flight. In its mildest manifestation, "flight" is avoidance. When we feel really threatened, some of us will physically run away. In the vast distance between those two extremes, are 100,000 unique versions of "flight" that individuals have created to handle the basic urge to run. The range for the "fighters" goes from passive-aggressive resistance to physical violence.

These are the first challenges of dealing with conflict: people's different styles of response, and the range at which people go into "conflict mode," which is the response or pattern of behaviour which individuals adopt automatically when they feel they are in a conflict.

In my first years of teaching, if I was confronted by an angry parent who had a complaint about my classroom, I was automatically in conflict mode. My response was avoidance. It took me a long time to realize that I was the only one having difficulty breathing in that situation. When I could train myself to stay out of conflict mode, it was easier to hear what the parents had to say. Many of them would not have considered our "conversation" a conflict. It was just a parent-teacher conference! Lighten up, eh!

Knowing that about myself was a huge help. I still had to work hard to manage my emotions, but it was much easier to do once I realized on a cognitive level that an aggressive style of communication is only that - a style. What one parent says gently and eloquently might have less merit than the abruptly delivered message of another. So I worked to stay out of conflict mode, where it is harder to think clearly, hear properly, and respond appropriately.

As a teacher in a regular classroom, I had to deal with conflict all the time. I felt it was negative. I saw it as something that took away from teaching time, forced me into a role I didn't like and was generally an ugly waste of my time. I drove home from work feeling frustrated beyond words: how could I eliminate the constant conflict in my classroom? I may as well have been thinking, How can I eliminate snow and cold from a Winnipeg winter?

I moved to Winnipeg as a young adult and was shocked and appalled by my first winter there. No one can prepare you for 35 degrees below zero and snow from October to March! I had two choices: sit in the basement all winter, polishing my canoe and muttering curses at the window, or learn how to enjoy a Winnipeg winter.

I joined a hockey team, which graciously allowed me to stay in spite of my skating skills. I learned to cross-country ski - barely. (I was really in it for the thermos of mint tea.) I tried curling, but frankly, all that sweeping confused me. Just vacuum once and be done with it. I eventually found ways to make winter fun, reasons to look forward to it. Winter never became my favourite season, but I stopped dreading it and focusing on it. I focused on what I could do with it.

After several frustrating years of working to "eliminate" conflict in my classroom, I began to see that it wasn't possible. As long as I had to have students in the room with me, there was going to be conflict! What I needed was a way to stop focusing on conflict itself and find ways to make use of it. I tried to see and remember the positive outcomes of dealing with conflicts. I focused on the progress kids showed in handling their conflicts and I tried to help them see conflict as normal and non-threatening. I tried hard to create positive models of appropriate interactions when a conflict arose between a student and myself. The classroom situation improved, but it was far from what I had envisioned in my idealistic, post-graduation imagination.

When I began working with at-risk kids, I had to delve a lot deeper into conflict. Understanding it more fully, especially with at-risk kids, was important, and I willingly learned all I could. Understanding conflict in myself was the most important, and I went there kicking and screaming!

One of the mottos at the Centre was: you can't ask a student to do something you are unwilling to do. So I began to get to know myself, and how I deal with conflict. I can't tell you how that process came about. I just know that when we talked about conflicts and situations with kids, we talked about ourselves: how we felt, if those feelings contributed to our responses, and what the kids might have felt coming from us in a conflict. Many times those conversations at work led to more conversations at home. A lot of soul-searching went on after school. I suspect if you are not really honest with yourself, you will always struggle in dealing with others. As I began to understand how I deal with conflict, I became more comfortable with it, became better at managing myself during conflict, and had a far better chance of understanding where the student was at.

This is not to say that I was running around looking for conflicts to escalate so that I could practise! On the contrary, most minor skirmishes in an average school day need to be circumvented. We have a job to do in our classrooms and that means ignoring a lot of quiet invitations to fight. Over the course of seven years at the RSC, I learned a lot of tricks for avoiding conflicts. While all kids are good at finding the right buttons to push with adults, some of these kids were the Einsteins of provocation!

The first thing I learned at the Centre was that there were some issues that just weren't worth worrying about. In a regular classroom, in days of old, I might have been irritated with a student who showed up every day without a pen or pencil. At the Centre, I had bigger fish to fry. Students showing up without lunches or proper winter clothing was worth dealing with. When I look back at some of the issues we used to stress about in the staff room in the early years of my career, I think, "There really is nothing so small that it can't be blown out of proportion."

Once I realigned my expectations, I began the long and sometimes painful task of learning how to avoid conflicts and power struggles. As I look back now, I think there are three main things that helped me: communication, flexibility, and relationship.

Communication

Communication is a huge area, and yet it can be the most specific and most narrow topic because every person sends and receives messages with his or her own personal twist. When you think of how individual communication is, it is a wonder any of us ever get anything across to each other. We all have our filters through which all messages must travel. The filter is comprised of the total sum of all our life experience to date, the emotions we have attached to those experiences, and the resulting interpretations we have made about our world and the people in it. If I asked every one of you to summarize what you've read so far, no two responses would be alike. Given the inherent challenges built into communication, making sure we are getting clear messages to and from damaged kids can be very difficult.

It didn't take long for me to realize that "concrete thinkers" were in our midst and misinterpreting a lot of messages during the course of their days. One day I looked out the window and commented that it was "raining cats and dogs." One boy knocked his desk over in his hurry to get to the window to witness such a gruesome miracle. Another boy came in from the playground after break one day looking genuinely puzzled and grabbed at the shoulder of his jacket to try to see his back. I found out later a disgruntled classmate had told him to "watch his back." There were dozens of examples of these misunderstandings. Imagine how confused such a student might be in a classroom filled with metaphors and the double meaning expressions of language. It was my experience that the adults with the simplest and clearest communication were the most effective in dealing with upset kids. When the chips are down and kids need help understanding something, whether it be an assignment or a confusing interaction with another person, they want clarity and simplicity, not colourful analogies and lyrical language.

We have all learned not to use sarcasm with students. Some of us struggle more than others. My own sense of humour, personal and professional, is always dancing dangerously at the borders of sarcasm. My strongest reminder to be careful with sarcasm came to me from a student. He was one of those concrete thinkers, and as we talked one day he said to me, "You know when you make comments sometimes and the kids all laugh? Well, you just sound mean to me." Ouch! A tough lesson, but I was motivated to do a better job of monitoring my "humour."

In an ideal world, we would have a perfect understanding of each of our students' communication styles and we would respond to each of them in the manner which best suited their needs. But while we still live here, in the real world, we need to be simple, clear, direct and kind in our communication. You can use the right words to achieve clarity, but the kindness is a different thing. It is about how we feel as we deliver the message. I read somewhere that communication is 55 percent facial expression, 38 percent tone of voice, and only 7 percent words!

One day a colleague at the Centre listened to a drama that occurred just beyond his sight, around a corner. A kindergarten student tripped and fell while running full throttle through an area he was not supposed to be in. The adult who found him lying on the floor crying over a skinned knee responded with appropriate words of comfort but her tone, so clear to the unobserved adult, was, "That's what you get for breaking the rules." What we're thinking is what they hear.

Communicating clear expectations to our students is vital. For those of us who teach children in the grades beyond primary, it is easy to forget that all the routines of school had to be taught at some point. We assume that when we ask for the class's attention, they know how to give it. I often think of the kindergarten teacher who asked her students to line up on the first day of school and then sighed tiredly as she watched the children running excitedly around the room, anxious to comply, but without the slightest notion about what it meant to "line up."

With each year of school, children are taught new routines and expectations. Most students will learn them easily and retain them from year to year, but a few do not. To avoid confusion, I found it helpful and often necessary to re-teach all those expectations as new kids entered my classroom. I told them precisely what I needed when I asked for their attention, told them what to do with their eyes, their mouths and their hands. I also told them why I thought it was best for them to look at the speaker, keep their mouth closed and make sure their hands were empty and still. That was only one example. I defined every expectation for them. I used clear, simple language and then checked to make sure everyone understood. Fortunately, being a talkative, easily distracted fidgeter myself gave me greater credibility in selling these helpful hints to the kids.

When we went on field trips, we previewed every aspect of the event, visualizing what it would look like. You would be amazed by how many different definitions of "stay together" there are.

Some examples of unclear communication I tripped over regularly.

I would say something like, "Dale, you definitely have to get that writing assignment done by the end of today." I meant that the writing assignment was a must, and then the rest of his work should be addressed as well. He heard or chose to hear, "All you have to do all day today is that writing assignment."

I said it was OK to snack quietly while they worked if they were really hungry. The kids heard, "It's OK to run to the store in the middle of class and get something to eat."

I said, "You guys can choose what game we play in gym today." They heard, "You can ransack the equipment room and run amok today."

Whatever I said, they interpreted to their advantage and then threw it back at me: "But you said we could!" Be very, very clear.

Once a conflict is on the horizon, communication becomes even more important. How I respond to an angry child can make the difference between a quick, easy solution and a full-blown power struggle. One of the best strategies I found for diffusing small situations was being careful to use I-messages rather than you-messages. This simply means to use yourself as the subject as much as possible: "I need you to sit down so we can start the lesson." "I'm feeling frustrated because I keep asking you to return to your desk and it feels as if you're just ignoring me."

Those are different messages than, "Sit down," or "You'd better start listening to me!"

Switching messages to I-format may sound stilted on paper. It may even sound stilted when you first try it aloud. I had been aware of this idea long before I arrived at the Centre, but I only used it occasionally when I felt I was heading into a conflict with someone, so, at times it probably did sound contrived. At the Centre, where many interactions with students were potentially explosive, I found myself using it frequently. It made a difference. At first I was aware only that it gave me some wiggle room. For example, if I said I felt a student was ignoring me, and he flew into a rage because I was "falsely accusing" him, I could diffuse the situation by pointing out that I didn't say he was ignoring me, I was just telling him how it felt for me. Even the best little lawyers among them got stumped with that one.

Eventually, and in part by observing interactions between other adults and students, I could see how effective it was. I could see that the difference in language created a difference in emotion - for the student and for the adult. I began to train myself to use I-language all the time. Soon, I didn't have to think about it. It became second nature and as it did, I assimilated it more completely into my own language patterns and it no longer sounded strange in my ears.

When I say that I-messages created different emotions in students and staff, I think of one student in particular. Dave was incredibly obstinate, and when he felt he had good cause, could outlast anyone in a standoff. Or a sitting-under-the-table-off. One day as he sat under his desk, refusing to move, or talk, or listen (he plugged his ears and sang loudly if anyone spoke to him) I decided to try a different approach. I would not talk to him, I'd talk to the teaching assistant. (Dave was also a hopeless busybody and lived for listening to adults when he wasn't supposed to.) I began to tell the TA, Terry, very honestly, how I was feeling about the situation with Dave. I told her why I was worried about this pattern of his from a teaching standpoint. Then I told her how it felt for me personally, to be trying so hard to help Dave without any results.

This was not an easy thing to do, but it goes back to what I said earlier: if we expect the kids to talk about their real feelings, we must be willing to do the same. Dave sat quietly for a while longer and then, abruptly, stated why he was mad. This started a dialogue and led to a happy ending. The big lesson for me that day was that my feelings played a role. When I tried to talk to Dave, he felt my frustration and his own negative feelings were triggered. Negative feelings lead to negative behaviours. When I focused on my reasons for feeling frustrated - my desire to help Dave - he felt that and responded to it.

The second big lesson of that day was the use of third-party communication. Talking to another adult in the presence of the student I was trying to reach became a tool I used almost daily in my time at the Centre.

After that, I was religious about I-messages. I blew it plenty, but I began every day committed to trying. I even started to touch my chest when I said "I." This helped me to remember that I was OK, and that I was separate from the students and their issues. I found it easy to get entwined with the emotions and issues of my students and that bit of physical grounding was my way of tangibly reminding myself: "You're you and I'm me and I don't have to feel your feelings to be empathetic." It also calmed me when I felt my counter-aggression getting into the act in response to aggressive students. I used it as a reminder to breathe and pay attention to what was happening in me.

The kids eventually picked up on that language and more than once I had I-messages sent right back at me! "I feel like you're picking on me when you tell me to hang up my coat all the time." I found that much easier to take (and address) than the more commonly used, "You're always picking on me, you *!@#*!"

We practised with the kids when we taught problem solving with peers. "If you tell Johnny how you felt when he called you a weenie, you may get a better result than just calling him another name or telling him to shut up." Some of the kids were remarkably good at doing just that, and small conflicts could be resolved before they became shouting matches, or worse.

The best thing about this little strategy is that it is easy to implement. You are the only one who needs to be on board, and you can try it for two weeks and see if it makes a difference. You don't have to start with sharing your feelings. Just change basic messages from "you" to "I" and note any changes.

If you're really skeptical, think about the public school system's all-time favourite you-message: "You apologize." Take a moment and think about someone saying that to you. How does it feel? Do you feel like apologizing? Do you feel good about yourself? Do you feel heard and validated? Do you feel like forgiving the person you're angry with?

The last thing I want to share about communication is the importance of being honest. Perhaps it seems silly that I would even mention something so basic, but in fact we all try to lie to students from time to time. We tell them we are not angry when we are. We tell them we think their work is great when it isn't. We tell them we like them when we don't. These are all well motivated, extremely damaging little lies. You simply cannot get those past street-wise kids. Their instincts about adults may be warped, but they are keen. If you want to connect with difficult kids, don't tell them you like them until you find something in them you genuinely like. Don't tell them you like their work until you really do. Tell them when you feel angry and tell them why. Show them that anger is normal - everyone feels it. Show them that not all angry adults are violent. Show them that you can do healthy, positive things with your feelings of anger. Show them they don't need to be afraid of anger in themselves or others. Make mistakes, and admit them. Tell the truth, even when it's hard.

Flexibility

Flexibility was the next lesson. Glory, that one hurt. I am a terminally well-organized person. You know the type: entire units prepared in advance, photocopying done, review and quiz prepared before the first lesson begins. I need structure. I want a schedule and I really, really want everyone to follow it. Please. The lessons of flexibility started as soon as I began teaching, as they must for every teacher. I learned to abandon doomed lesson plans and change direction in midstream. I learned to negotiate and compromise. It is, after all, a matter of survival in the classroom. I was far more relaxed and flexible after eight years of teaching. Then I arrived at the Centre and "flexibility" took on a whole new meaning for me. Flexibility is simply a wide range of motion. I had to do some moving all right, but most of it had to happen in my head.

"Structured flexibility" became one of my mental mantras. (That and, "bob and weave" when things were flying around the classroom.) It was very important that our kids had predictability. Some of them could not handle change. We used a timetable in our classroom and the kids were quite attached to it. If there was going to be a change in the schedule, some kids needed 24 hours' notice to get used to the idea. They needed to know that they would hang their coat in the same place each morning, follow a schedule through the day, eat lunch at the same time, have gym on the same day, have a field trip every other Friday. I could see how they all relaxed into the structure - even the easygoing ones. They also needed some predictability and routine in relationships. They loved to ask me if I went swimming before school. They loved to know that Bob would bellow hello to them every morning. They needed to know that if they made the effort to get to school, the same group of "safe" adults would be there to meet them. These things were important.

The trick is to get maximum flexibility within consistent and predictable structure. For example, every morning at 9:00, we had Group. Sometimes we played a game, sometimes we had show and tell, sometimes we had specific lessons from our social/emotional teaching kit, sometimes we discussed an issue or incident from the previous day, and sometimes we just sat around and gossiped. But at 9:00 a.m. Monday through Friday, we were in Group.

At 9:30 it might be math class. Some did math on the computer, some did it out of a textbook, some used workbooks or worksheets, some played math games or used math manipulatives. Sometimes we did some crazy project that could just barely be construed as math (with enough imagination). But we all did math from 9:30 to 10:00.

If a student couldn't face the textbook, he could negotiate to do some other math. He might even be able to help a younger student with math. He could probably work a deal as long as he stayed within the boundaries of "math."

Being flexible with kids avoided many power struggles. The first thing I would suggest to anyone on this topic is to be flexible in your vision. Sometimes we set a goal and the end result looks a certain way to us, as does the process of how to reach the goal. Sometimes the kids have their own vision of how to get where you want them to go. Be flexible with that. If you want them to do math, that is a good clear boundary. Within that, does it really matter how the goal is met? If they do the math while sitting on the floor, is the math less done? If they do it on the blackboard, or in pencil crayon, or while listening to headphones, is the math less done?

Many people misread flexibility to mean having no boundaries. To me, flexibility means that the boundaries do not move, but the choices within the boundaries increase. Wherever you set your boundaries in your classroom, at-risk kids will spend most of their time right at the edges. It is important that those boundaries stay put.

When Jason bumped into the boundary during math, and refused to do "any math today," we simply reminded him that the choice was his. If he was okay with the consequences of his choice on his report card, he was welcome to sit quietly at his desk and not bother anyone else. However, we pointed out to Jason that there wasn't actually much math to be done and that he could do it himself, or with an adult. He could do it at his desk, or join me at my desk, or sit at the table, or move into the Quiet Room. He could do a few multiplication flashcards first to get in the mood, or he could just relax and see if he changed his mind. We left him alone to contemplate the myriad of options and soon he chose one and got to work.

Giving kids choices within the boundaries is very important. Many of our kids at the Centre had huge control issues. Either they were in charge at home and didn't fancy relinquishing power at school, or they felt completely powerless at home and took every opportunity at school to feel "in control." Giving as many options as possible gave these kids the opportunity to comply without losing face or feeling threatened.

It is also necessary to give kids time and space and dignity. If you order someone to get to work and then stand in front of her and wait for her to comply, you are inviting a conflict. If you do that with an at-risk student, you are inviting a trip to Emergency. Make a request, and leave them to do it in their own time. You know there is a time limit, but they don't need to know it.

I kept a small, full basket of markers on my desk. There were many colours. My first response to any student refusing to work was to walk to his desk with the markers, and, totally ignoring whatever declarations of strike were forthcoming, ask him what colour of pen he would like to use. Amazing but true, this was often enough of a distraction to make them forget the strike action and change their focus. I had many kids drop off in mid-sentence to start rummaging through the marker basket. Sometimes refusing to work is just an old habit.

Kids like to bargain. If you think making a deal with a kid is a sell-out or a capitulation of some kind, you may not want to work with difficult kids. When I first began teaching, I felt that making a deal with a student sent all the wrong messages: that the adult was not in control when he or she should be, that the student could manipulate the adult, that the student was not learning to accept direction. When I had worked at the Centre for a wee while, I turned into Monty Hall. I negotiated about the precise number of math questions that would constitute "enough" math. I made deals about skipping break and leaving ten minutes early. I made deals to get kids to eat their lunch, come to school, not run away from home. I had a goal and we used the kid's route to get there. Along the way, the student learned that adults did listen and could show compassion. They learned that they had some control over their lives. They learned the power of communication skills. And I slowly got kids on board, built relationships, figured out how they thought and learned, and didn't need to make deals to reach goals anymore.

Relationships

Every teacher's greatest asset in the classroom is the ability to connect with kids. Even if I had the communication skills perfected and was totally flexible, if I had no relationship with a kid, I had little hope of avoiding a conflict with one who was looking for a fight.

Before we dive in here, let me paint a little scene for you. The setting is a dentist's office. She is a lovely dentist, kind and gentle. In the examination chair is a patient. Oh look, it's me. The dentist has not started the examination, she is just chatting with me. Or trying to.

"How are you today, Monica?"

"Fine."

"Are you enjoying this great weather?"

"Yes."

"How is school going?"

"Fine."

"Are you planning a vacation for the holidays?"

"Yes."

"I'm going to start now. Are you feeling ready?"

Frown, mumble, whimper, fight back tears.

This is exactly what I am like at the dentist's office. It starts as soon as I pull into the parking lot. I am terrified of going to the dentist and have been since childhood. ("What's that, dear? No, you couldn't possibly be feeling that. Just relax.")

As an adult, I have chosen my dentists very carefully, worked hard to overcome my irrational fears, done relaxation exercises, used breathing techniques, tried it all! I have improved dramatically, but even on my best days at the dentist, most people would find me unrecognizable from my usual self.

The only reason I can get myself to the dentist at all, is because of the relationship I had with a former dentist, Patty. She came and sat with me in the waiting room and chatted about whatever for a bit. Then she told me what she was going to do when we went "to the back." We talked specifically about how I was feeling and we went in when I felt ready. Simple connections that made it possible for me to try to cooperate.

If you only ever saw me at the dentist's office, I guarantee that you would not like me. When you are getting to know the "difficult" kids in your class, remember that school is probably their least favourite environment. This is where they are at their worst; they are nervous, maybe even flat out terrified. They can't think clearly, they don't operate the same way they do when they are relaxed. I have had many kids describe this to me. One child's story in particular stuck with me. She looked at me tearfully and said, "Every day, as soon as I turn the corner and I can see the school, my stomach starts to hurt."

If you really want to connect with these kids, find ways to meet them on their turf. Go watch them shoot hoops at noon in the gym. Walk with them around the neighbourhood, away from the school. Let them tell you about hockey, building models, going to garage sales with Grandpa, summer camp, fishing. Find a place, if only in your shared imagination, where you can see them at their best - where they look straight at you with confidence, and their eyes are bright and they speak more clearly and quickly; where you can get a glimpse of who they really are. Then hang on to that image, that feeling, and don't lose it. You will need it when they are screaming at you later on.

If you are the kind of person who connects well with kids, building relationships is natural and you probably don't even think about it. When you meet up with disconnected kids, it is a different story. Many of the students who came to us had no trust in adults. They were wary and suspicious. These kids are in all classes. I had dealt with difficult children before - been forced to consciously think about ways to connect with a student. At the Centre however, the exception was the child who bonded easily with adults. I was constantly struggling to find ways to reach kids who were practised and adept at keeping everyone at arm's length.

Let me begin with the obvious. Names. I made a point of knowing each student's name before he or she arrived. I tried not to let the introduction happen. I greeted them immediately with, "This must be ... I'm happy you're here."

But, I did not let them know that I knew anything beyond their names. Kids who have had difficulty in school have a fat file and most of them know it. I read those files and pretended I did not know a thing about their family, their previous history, or why they were referred to the Centre. All that was their story to tell. The first time a kid suspected that I knew something beyond what she had shared with me, she shut down on me completely and it was a long road back to rebuild the trust.

The power of names is huge. I can't even explain why it is so. I was playing in a hockey game one night and a conflict arose between two players right at the end of the game. It carried over afterwards and as the rest of us shook hands, one of the players involved grew more and more agitated. She seemed determined to provoke my teammate into a fight. As she yelled and swore, she called my teammate a name to which my friend replied, "My name is Barbara." That was all. She made eye contact and calmly stated her name. The other woman stopped in mid-tirade and looked slightly confused for a second. I wondered if she was contemplating introducing herself, as well! She turned and walked away and that was the end of it. It is much easier to rant and rave at a nameless, unidentified body than at a person with a name.

Students exist in a system. In any system, it is a danger if individuality becomes lost: I am just one of 30 kids. I am one of the sixth graders. I am in the Bluebird reading group. It's good to identify with a group, but it's critical to retain your individual identity. This is true for all kids in all classrooms. Learn those names as quickly as humanly possible.

Remember playground duty at your first school on your first day? I do. I knew exactly zero names and "Hey you" just did not cut it. It was frustrating and frightening. The students knew in the first 30 seconds that I didn't know who they were and they were on me like wolves!

As a substitute teacher one year, I learned this lesson over and over. I needed to know their names (preferably their real ones) and they needed to know mine. One class in particular was taking me for a ride, so I stood in front of them quietly without responding to their yelling and laughing and general mayhem. After a few minutes they got curious about why I was just standing there watching them, and they quieted down enough for me to be heard. As soon as I had that opening, I said, "My name is Monica." When no one threw anything, I continued.

"I have two dogs, Thai and Bro ..." I yacked non-stop about my personal life until one of them interrupted with a question, which I tried to answer honestly. By the end of our time together, we had reached an uneasy truce and actually did most of the work left by the teacher. Again, it is much easier to abuse a nameless entity than someone with a name. A name is personhood, especially a first name.

Nicknames are surprisingly powerful also. Friends give them to each other. It provides a feeling of intimacy and connection. Kids who end up in special programs due to their behaviour rarely have cute nicknames that their peers or teachers have given them. Sometimes they have slightly scary ones like Lighter Boy. And many times the kids in the class have dubbed them, but with a hateful name that sets them off, and was probably created for that purpose. I found that having a pet name for each kid made them feel special. Some names caught on and everyone at the Centre used them. Some were only used privately when talking one on one. In addition to each kid's special nickname, I had a tendency to call them all "Sparky" or "Junior" at times. One new student got quite offended when I called him Junior and then used the same name with another student later on. One of the students who had been around a while explained to him, "She calls everyone Junior. That's how you know she likes you." A caution: use a pet name with all of them or none of them. They will notice.

There is also power in acknowledgement. A simple greeting can be a big thing. As you know by now, I used to swim in the mornings before school. At the city pool I used, the receptionist for one period was a particularly friendly woman named Donna. Every morning as I came into the building, I was greeted with a cheerful "Good morning!" As I left, I heard "Have a good day!" I loved that - no matter how cold and dark and miserable it was outside, I felt warm the moment I saw her smile every morning. I didn't realize how important her salutations had become until one morning when I left the pool. She was talking on the phone and couldn't give me my usual send-off.

I was already halfway across the lobby and she hadn't said anything. I suddenly realized that I had begun slowing down. I was walking slower and slower, to give her time to hang up and tell me to have a good day. My slowing was unconscious, but when I became aware of what I was doing and why, I realized just how powerful those greeting rituals can be.

My first year at the RSC, I worked there only half-time. The other half I taught regular classes at the junior high school, where I had run the transition program the previous year. Because I was only half-time, I did not have a classroom at the junior high. I moved around, meeting my classes in other people's rooms and pushing textbooks and supplies around the halls on a little cart.

I had two Grade 7 social studies classes. They were fairly well matched in ability, number and general make-up. However, I found I had many more classroom management problems with one class than the other. At first, I couldn't identify the problem. It wasn't as though there were difficult kids in one class that were causing all the disruptions. There were the usual number in both groups! One class was just more difficult to get settled, more talkative, had more minor clashes with one another. I examined my timetable to look for a clue. I found one. One class was always scheduled either first thing in the morning or right after lunch. I had lots of time to wheel my cart to the room, and get myself organized before the students arrived. With the other class, I was always rushing just to get there on time. They were often there before me. With class A, I was at the door, saying hello, making eye contact with each student, and just connecting. I could detect rumblings, moods, potential conflicts, and could help calm the waters before I tried to teach. Class B didn't get that. I reworked my route and timing a bit (translation: no pee break), and tried to get to class B ahead of them. I didn't have time to organize materials, but I was at the door, smiling and welcoming them, making person-to-person contact, rather than standing up in front of them, remote and unconnected, trying to get a whole group of kids on-side with me.

I once did an inservice with the bus drivers of our school division on the topic of dealing with conflict. When we talked about building relationships, there was plenty of skepticism about doing so with a kid when your main contact was the three seconds it took to board the bus and the three seconds to disembark. The discussion centered on the difficult kids with whom six seconds a day is never going to be enough. I wish we had spent more time talking about the fact that those drivers were accomplishing the six-second miracle with 95 percent of the students who rode their buses. The only tools they had were the use of names and greetings, and most of them were managing to connect really well.

By the way, if you try to greet a student and get no response, don't give up. He might be unable to respond, yet. Or he might be trying to prove to himself that his irrational beliefs about adults are correct. When you give up and stop saying hello, you get put in the "adults who don't like me" category and then the student can treat you however he wishes without feeling badly. You never know why students can't or won't respond - but you can't assume that they never will.

Billy was a beautiful little boy who came to the Centre in Grade 3. He had physically assaulted enough adults at his home school to be removed indefinitely. He had been horribly abused and was a shell-shocked, terrified, and understandably vicious little guy. He was non-responsive at first. I remember him spending a lot of time sitting in the far corner of rooms, his back safely touching both walls and watching everyone warily with darting, angry eyes. Every morning when he arrived, he would take the Lego box to the common area and sit in his corner and play. And every single morning, the director at the time, Sylvia, would smile at him and say, "Good morning, Billy!" Every morning, there was no response. One morning, Billy arrived earlier than usual and took his place in the corner. Sylvia, unaware that he was there, walked quickly through the common area to deliver a message to the classroom and didn't notice him. As she reached the classroom door, she heard an unfamiliar and reproachful little voice say quietly, "Good morning, Sylvia."

Don't assume that your greeting, your effort to connect, is not getting through just because you are not getting a response.

We all have our own ways of connecting with others. Know what works best for you and practise those skills vigilantly. A relationship is worth more than all the pedagogical expertise in the world.

Communication, flexibility and relationships were the three things I found helped me the most in my efforts to avoid conflicts with students. Perhaps I should also mention forgiveness. I once told the kids that every day was a fresh start - that I had a magic button in my head that completely erased the previous day. One day, a boy who had had a very rough Monday, came in on Tuesday morning and after hanging around at a distance unable to make eye contact, finally approached me to ask sheepishly if I could "please push that button in my head." It took me a minute to figure out what he was talking about, and then I ceremoniously pantomimed a quick mechanical procedure on my own head and we started Tuesday with a laugh together. I couldn't have imagined that on Monday afternoon!

Finally, the far more difficult part - forgiveness of myself. I blew it all the time. I went home many nights and looked back over the day and thought about how I could have handled things better, where I might have diffused a situation, when I got trapped in a power struggle I should have avoided. It was hard to give myself room to fail but I figured if the kids could forgive me - if they could still show up for school and let me try again - then I could forgive myself, too. If you work with at-risk kids, remember to be as gentle with yourself as you are with them.

Chapter 5

Dealing with Conflict

Seeing past the armour

S o here we are. We have honed our skills, built wondrous relationships and there are still conflicts. Some of them are just not going to be avoided no matter what we do.

As I write, I think fondly of all the people I have fought with in my career - so many kids, some teachers, the odd parent, a few administrators - ah, so many lovely memories. Quite honestly, I don't have negative feelings when I look back at dealing with conflict. That is a gift that I have taken from the Centre - most days now, I don't see conflict as a negative thing.

But the person I fought with the most was, without question, my boss, Sylvia. We both claimed that we fought more with each other than with anyone else in our lives. Sometimes it was a quick, heated conversation that took five minutes, ended with the usual hug, and was over. Sometimes, it went on for days, requiring two or three sessions of discussion. These were difficult and unpleasant, but they were always resolved with a positive outcome. When we argued about our differing ideas about what should happen with a student's program, I usually lost, but I always learned something (although I may not have been prepared to articulate or even admit it at the time).

Looking back now, I try to understand why I had so many conflicts with Sylvia. I think, in part, it was because it was a safe place to speak my mind without having to censor my every thought. I was not afraid that it would damage or destroy our friendship. I think we both knew, when we dove in, that the final result would be positive. We weren't afraid of the process because we had faith in the outcome. And I don't mean an outcome about who was right and who was wrong. I mean that we were both 100 percent sure that however the conflict ended, we would still be friends. There was definitely a hug waiting at the end of the muck. We just had to persevere and wade through it.

I think this is one of the first things we need to work at with kids who are prone to conflict. Conflict is scary. When kids are emotionally flooded, their behaviour is running directly off the "feelings battery." With at-risk kids, the behaviour will look as though they are angry, but they are likely scared. To get more reasonable behaviour from them, to address the problem, kids in conflict will need to be reassured that the process will have a positive outcome in some form. For them to engage in resolving conflict, they need the same confidence that I had with Sylvia - they need to know that whatever happens during the process, they will not lose their relationship with you.

The first few times you work through a conflict with a kid, you need to tell him or her this: regardless of what you tell me when you're upset, I will still like you and be your friend. When you walk that talk a few times, you won't have to say it any more, and the kids will be less fearful and therefore, perhaps, a little more reasonable.

Being confident in the process and helping the kids feel it too, is the first necessity. The second is accepting this basic truth: you have no control over the other person in a conflict, regardless of their age, size, experience, or abilities. None. You only have control over yourself. Get comfortable with that idea.

I found my best hope for handling conflict effectively was to understand as much about it as I could. I learned about the natural stresses that create conflict - developmental, economic or physical, psychological and reality stresses.[4] Once I knew about them, I could recognize their influence in situations.

Developmental stress refers to all the anxiety we all feel as we go through the natural stages of our life. Adolescence is packed with it. The beginning of independence is often a time of conflict with parents, as young people struggle with the realization that adults are not infallible. This is an underlying contributor to most conflicts between teens and their parents and is often carried over to relationships between teens and teachers.

Economic or physical stress is often evident in our classrooms. Families living near or in poverty have the stresses of hunger, anxiety about basic necessities, physical illness due to lack of appropriate shelter, clothing, nutrition or health care. Parents who spend every ounce of energy on survival have little left for nurturing their children. I, with my comfortable middle class upbringing, had little idea of how many kids show up for school every day unable to concentrate on anything but an empty tummy.

We had one student, Darren, who came to us in second grade. He would be sitting working and suddenly show signs of agitation. By the time one of us got to him, he could be out of control - throwing things at people, screaming, trying to break things. On one of these occasions, we had to carry Darren into the Quiet Room and I held him while he screamed and tried to hit me. When he was finally quiet, I noticed that I was hungry from the stress of the situation. I asked him if he was hungry and he nodded tearfully. We had a snack together and played a game of Connect Four. When he was finally ready, we began to problem solve.

He seemed to be more agitated than usual with the process, and I stopped and just sat with him for a bit. Eventually, he said, "Why are we problem solving? I already told you why I got mad."

Confused, I asked him to tell me again, and he said, "Because I was hungry."

Darren is an extreme case, but the fact is that sometimes, basic unmet needs are at the heart of, or may contribute to, conflict situations.

Psychological stress refers to the damaging messages that we hear, take in and internalize. Kids with behaviour difficulties have received more than their share of these. They've been told that they are bad and/or stupid, that they are the reason for a marital breakdown, that their behaviour is destroying their family or their classroom, that they are failures, and that they are worthless. These messages create negative feelings that fuel negative behaviour. Imagine getting up every day and believing those messages about yourself. How could you possibly function normally? Many times I have asked kids why they did something and been told, "Because I'm bad."

As this phenomenon became real for me when I witnessed it in child after child, I began to listen more closely to the messages that ran on my own internal tape. Which comments of others did I allow to get through? I found that I had a tendency to replay the negative ones and disregard the positives. As I looked around my classroom, I began to change that tape. I made a very conscious choice to stop "filtering out" the compliments of others and to give myself more positive messages.

You can't stand in a pit of self-deprecation and yell up to the surface to tell the kids they should feel good about themselves.

Reality stress is created by the reality of life: sometimes things go wrong. For most of us, these things are manageable. When we get a flat tire, or the computer crashes, or we find an ink stain on our favourite slacks, we will handle it without a major meltdown.

In school, things go wrong all the time. Sometimes binders get knocked off desks accidentally and the rings pop open and papers scatter everywhere. When this happens, most kids will have a very minor negative reaction before getting down to dealing with it. A kid who was up all night listening to parents fighting about money, who is in conflict with his parents over curfew, who is hungry, or embarrassed by acne and can't stand being the focal point of attention … a very different reaction may come from that student.

Remember Jason, standing on his desk yelling obscenities? That situation started with developmental stress - adjusting to a junior high school and being unable to read the timetable. It was fueled by reality stress when he was late, and ignited by the psychological stress of his reputation as a weak student. He chose to look like a "badass" rather than an "idiot" with the wrong book.

I also became aware of these stresses in my own life. If I, or someone in my family was dealing with stress, that affected me at work and I needed to be aware of and monitor it. Probably my most common pre-existing stress was lack of sleep. I need eight hours to be at my best. I can feel the difference if I have seven hours and anything under six starts to be dangerous for people around me. My awareness of this taught me to be a little more flexible with kids with circles under their eyes. I knew how they felt. More importantly, I needed to be aware of my fatigue all day and calculate it into my reactions to situations. Many times, I had to remind myself that I was tired, probably a little cranky. If Sparky had snuck up behind me yesterday and yelled boo in my ear, I would probably have thought it was funny, but on the bad day, the line of punishments running through my head were likely inappropriate for the situation.

Classrooms are full of potential sources of stress: being on time, having all the correct materials, remembering assignments and being capable of understanding and completing them, getting along with peers, following rules, living up to the many expectations of your teachers, parents and yourself. Some kids are stressed just entering the classroom and it will not take much to set off a conflict with them. What type of stress our students are dealing with on a daily basis is important information for us to have. When I problem-solved with students, I often found red flags that were tied to those pre-existing stresses and were simply touched off by the visible incident we were discussing.

As I mentioned earlier, I learned about conflict styles. It was valuable to be able to recognize the style of someone else, but critical that I understood my own. I learned that I am basically assertive until I get emotionally charged and then I have the potential to slide towards aggressive. (I've come a long way from my days in the "passive" category.) The compatibility of styles in a conflict is something the helping adult must keep in mind. If you find conflicts end quickly and easily with a certain student but keep returning, you may need to take a closer look at the conflict styles involved. A passive student will back off immediately and do whatever is necessary to smooth the waters, but he/she is resolving nothing.

Two aggressive types will have a lot of difficulty resolving conflicts. If one is an adult, guess who needs to change his or her style? Keeping this information in the front of my mind rather than the back helped me in all conflict situations. When we are in conflict, it is harder to think clearly and we need to practise being aware of what is happening, even in the midst of the melee. I know that sometimes I get louder in conflict, so I tell myself to lower my voice. If I am bigger than the other participant in the conflict, I sit down. I have a tendency to point or cross my arms, so I put my hands in my pockets. This may sound silly, but it is just practising awareness. Once you can manipulate all these factors in the midst of a conflict, you will have two positive outcomes: you will have positively affected the current conflict, and you will be prepared for more difficult challenges in being "aware" in the midst of conflict. To be specific, you will be ready to monitor and manage your own feelings of anger and aggression even in the heat of battle.

Why do adults get angry and aggressive? I can read your mind and your response is too vague: Yes, the kids piss us off, but why? We are all aware that other people's behaviour cannot create behaviour in us. Their behaviour can influence what we think and therefore feel. Our feelings are a determinate in our response, but no one else can make us act a certain way. So what is happening with our thoughts and feelings to create aggression in us when we are dealing with difficult kids?

I have already touched on the first reason that adults become angry: they are under the weather physically. If you are tired or sick, you just don't have the same reserves of energy and patience that you normally would. I have said to a student halfway through dealing with him, "You are probably getting more than you deserve here, because I feel crappy. I'll let someone else handle this." For the few times I verbalized it, I thought it many more times. Sometimes I just said to myself, "You're tired and cranky. Take about 30 percent off the top of your reaction before you talk to Junior."

Sometimes kids stumble onto our personal issues. I remember very clearly the day young Albert did this. He had to stay at his desk during break time and as usual did so with a great deal of moaning and complaining. He was never shy to express his displeasure with staff and regulations at the Centre, and so I was accustomed to tuning him out. However, on this particular occasion, his tactic was to compare his plight (no break) to that of someone suffering with cancer. He went on for a bit and then said that I, specifically, made him suffer worse than someone with cancer. During the course of his tirade, I had gone from bored to incensed in about one minute. I opened my mouth to unleash on him, when I realized that I was barely under control and left the room.

As I walked outside I was very upset about how angry I had become. Albert had just been his usual self. The difference was that he had unwittingly stumbled onto a personal issue for me. He did not know that every day after school I was going to the hospital and sitting by the bedside of a loved one dying of cancer. Terry, the teaching assistant, seeing the look on my face before I left the room, knew what was going on in my personal life and quickly sized up what had happened. She turned the situation into a "teachable moment" and told Albert what was going on in my life and why I was so upset. Albert learned to consider the impact of his words on others and I learned that personal issues can be an explosive component in classroom dynamics.

While we are on the subject of kids wandering into landmines, what about our triggers? We all have little things that set us off for no apparent reason. Immediately, I can think of two for myself: being snapped with a wet towel and being told to relax. I don't know why, but I am angry immediately when either of these two things occurs. Thankfully, the first doesn't come up too often in a classroom, but the second made very regular appearances in my school life. It didn't even have to be the word relax. Even the tone could set me off. An adolescent can tell you to relax with any number of words, looks or grunts.

"Take it easy, would ya?"

"OK. Whatever."

"Ho-ly."

"What's your problem?"

Try it. If you say it with the right intonation, almost anything can sound like, Relax!

I had been aware before I came to the Centre that this was a trigger for me (the year of subbing had made it abundantly clear). When I got to the RSC and began hearing it regularly, I needed to take action. I don't remember formulating a plan. One day I just confessed. I told a colleague that being told to relax just sent me right through the roof. Being the caring professional that he was, he immediately began telling me to relax at every opportunity. At first I was predictably annoyed; annoyed every time he said it, obviously, and annoyed that he was using my confession against me. However, I soon got used to it. I became a bit desensitized to it. Next, all the staff took great glee in telling me to relax, and what could I possibly do but laugh? Soon, when the kids told me to relax, some adult would echo it quickly. ("Yeah, Monica, why don't you relax?"), and it became a way of diffusing me before I even got going. Now, I am happy to report, you can tell me to relax and it will just make me smile. Most days.

We all create roles for ourselves. We see ourselves in certain ways and that identity helps form the boundaries around our predictable behaviours. For example, a person who sees himself as dignified will hardly ever be found riding a mechanical bull. As teachers, we do the same thing. We can be angered when we feel pushed beyond the boundaries of our comfort zone as defined by our role.

I always saw myself as a great classroom manager. My classrooms were usually fairly quiet, and always under control. As a result, my students missed out on some good stuff. I could barely bring myself to do group work and projects because that was a harder atmosphere for me to keep orderly and organized. I didn't even like going to the library. Obviously, I did all these things, but I was outside my comfort zone and was far quicker to react negatively to students when we were in these configurations as opposed to safely in our classroom, everyone at his or her own desk. As I began to be more aware of this, I made a conscious effort to do more group work and practised being more relaxed while doing it. With time, I improved and was less irritable in less structured situations.

At the Centre, with the luxury of full-time assistants in the classroom, I often gave those tasks away. Science projects became the domain of Peter or Terry - they could both laugh when it was loud and raucous and there was gunk running all over the table. And from the safety of my desk I could see how engaged the kids were and how much they were learning.

As adults, we can also become angry when a child is behaving in a way that offends our personal value system. We all have certain core values and beliefs, and when a child operates outside of those in any way, we feel uncomfortable. If they are far enough from our values to really offend us, we may feel angry.

Imagine that you have two girls in your class, Betty and Wilma. Wilma is a good student. She completes all her work on time and does a pretty good job. She is always present, always on time, always in possession of all necessary materials. She is clean and well-dressed, has nice manners and a pleasant personality.

Betty misses a fair bit of school, is sometimes late and usually hands in messy or incomplete assignments. She is often missing supplies and is usually scowling and churlish. Her personal hygiene is, in your opinion, not very good.

One day, after you have delivered yet another inspired lesson and given an assignment, Betty and Wilma both approach your desk.

"I need a little help with the first question, please," says Wilma.

"I don't get it," growls Betty.

Who do you feel like helping? They are both at your desk because they want to learn. They are both motivated to do the assignment and are requesting your assistance in their own styles. Why is there a difference in your emotional response to these two girls? Because

Wilma's personal values about work ethic, hygiene, manners, etc, are very close to your own. Betty is offending your value system all over the place and it makes you understandably uncomfortable.

When Betty and Wilma approach my desk, I need to remind myself that Betty is just as motivated to learn and just as deserving of my help and attention as cute little Wilma. I am not saying there isn't room for some teaching and possibly some change on Betty's part. But the teaching needs to come from a place of wanting to offer her some skills that might assist her in society, not from a place of thinking she needs to change because she is not good enough! We develop our core values very early, largely through our family. Trying to change someone's core values can send them a very negative message about their parents. That is dangerous territory.

Sometimes our values create our triggers. I have not yet talked to a group of teachers or teaching assistants who did not list "spitting" amongst their triggers. For our generation, spitting is a sign of disrespect and contempt. It does not carry the same meaning any more and our students think nothing of it. While they are just picking another annoying behaviour out of their bag of tricks, we are incensed because that particular one is so loaded with meaning - for us.

I value honesty. It is important to me. I worked with kids who really didn't get what I meant. Honesty was just a choice to them: should I tell the truth in this situation? Nope - too risky. This was the hardest one for me to handle. I got angry when kids lied to me because they were offending the most sacred part of my value system. They didn't know that. I had to remember that, or my righteous indignation was just an unexpected and somewhat mystifying reprimand to them. It didn't carry any weight with them because they didn't share my values. I had to be aware of when my values were coming into play and temper my responses accordingly.

Another reason that adults get angry is good old Counter-Aggression. Counter aggression means that when one person is aggressive, the person at whom the aggression is directed will, most likely unconsciously, mirror that behaviour. It is a natural phenomenon. Watch an argument between two people: the first person gets louder, the second gets louder. The first moves forward, so does the second. The first yells, the second yells right back.

When aggressive kids get "in our face," our natural tendency is to give it right back to them! Unaware adults can mirror the behaviour of an aggressive child without noticing what they are doing. This generally leads to power struggles that no one wins.

With understanding, and lots of practice, we can be aware of our feelings of counter aggression and make our decisions about how to respond. Self-talk becomes critical as feelings of counter aggression kick in. For me, with my short fuse, self-talk was important. Occasionally, I would realize I was getting angry, stop myself in mid-sentence, mutter, "Counter aggression is your friend, Monica," and walk away.

The last and largest reason for adult anger/aggression is being trapped in the Conflict Cycle.[5]

The conflict cycle begins with a stressful incident. What the student says to him/herself about that incident creates feelings that lead to inappropriate or ineffective behaviour. Adult reaction can create more stress for the child, increasing negative feelings and fueling more inappropriate behaviour. Worse behaviour brings stronger reaction from the adult and around and around it goes.

The key ingredient that makes conflict more volatile with difficult kids is their self-concept.

Like the kids I've talked about, many children believe that they are bad, that adults are all out to get them, that nothing good can ever happen to them, that they don't deserve happiness, that they are the cause of all the difficulty and pain that they have experienced in their lives. These are just a few beliefs. It is this self-concept that determines the reaction to stress more than anything else. The truth is irrelevant. An intelligent child who believes he is "stupid" will perform poorly in academics.

I have seen this played out in front of me so many times, I no longer doubt its truth. It makes me sad to think of all the times that I told students that they were "capable of more" without providing a way to help them believe it. I may as well have told them they could perform brain surgery.

At the beginning of the conflict cycle, when a stressful incident occurs, a healthy, well-adjusted child will give himself an appropriate message about what it means, and the resulting feelings will be commensurate with the event. The choice of action to take, or the behaviour, will reflect those feelings. No problem.

An at-risk child experiencing the same stressful incident might believe that adults are all adversarial and potentially dangerous. When an initial incident occurs, she sounds an internal alarm and thinks about what could happen, based on her irrational belief about adults. Her thoughts create negative feelings, which fuel a negative response. A very different scenario develops here.

This takes us back to the importance of being positive with the kids. They must begin to believe positive things about themselves to even have a chance at responding appropriately to stressful situations.

I had one student for the better part of two years, who was eleven years old when he came to us. This guy could not handle upsets! If his team lost in gym, if he made a mistake on a spelling quiz, if his lunch had something he didn't like - any little thing - it could set him off. It usually ended the same way every day - Calvin on the floor of the Quiet Room, breaking something. He almost always destroyed his own stuff: his binders, calculators, Walkman, tapes, pens and pencils, etc. It looked as though he was trying to punish himself. He would insist, through any problem-solving attempts, that he was just mad about what had happened and this was how he dealt with it. End of discussion.

After a while I began to speculate to myself (out loud, in front of Calvin) about what might make a guy punish himself that way. I named for Calvin all the hurts he was unable to name himself. I "gave him permission" to be upset about his situation and told him that if it were me, I would be feeling abandoned, hurt and very angry. We had this one-sided conversation many times. One day, I suggested that Calvin write a letter to his absent mother and tell her how he felt. (He still refused to acknowledge there was any problem at all, but he never interrupted me when I did my speculating.)

I told him he could do what he wanted with the letter - keep it, mail it, share it with one of the staff at school, share it with his guardians, or destroy it. I left him alone for almost an hour. Every time I peeked in the window, he was absorbed in his letter. He even made a good copy. He finally came out on his own, announced he wanted to get back to work in the classroom, and did not want to talk anymore. (Translation: Not one word about that letter, lady - I'm warning you!)

I went into the office where he had been and there was the letter, ripped into pieces and piled neatly on the coffee table. I took it home and taped it back together. Then I had one of my longer cries. In the letter I read, "You better get back home. You better not find a boyfriend over there and get pregnant and have another mistake."

Imagine what the world looks like to those who don't believe they have a place in it, who believe they are just someone's mistake. No wonder he couldn't talk himself through minor upsets - he had no positive feelings about himself to draw on.

Back to the cycle: a student experiences a stressful incident, irrational beliefs trigger negative feelings, which fuel some negative behaviour. Then the adult responds. Right here is our best opportunity to avoid a conflict. If we react negatively, the student's anxiety increases, he responds with more or even worse negative behaviour. Now the adult is probably getting more upset and the cycle is off and running and will likely soon be out of control.

If, at that first show of negative behaviour, we can ignore it and let the child de-stress on his own, or if we can help him with whatever initial incident caused the stress originally, we might avoid the conflict. Often, the child's negative reaction to the first source of stress can't be ignored. How we handle it will determine the course of events.

In my first year of working with at-risk students at the junior high school, I observed a perfect example of the conflict cycle getting revved up and out of control. It occurred in a grade seven math class during the first few days of school in September.

It was the first day of math and the teacher was telling the class how the course would work, what evaluation would be used and how marks would be calculated. A student started talking to his neighbour and the teacher asked him to be quiet. The student gave a cheeky reply to which the teacher responded more sternly, again asking him to be quiet. The student got even cheekier and the frustrated teacher told him if he couldn't be quiet, he would have to leave the classroom. The student jumped up, swore, chucked his pencil across the room and stormed out. This is not a terribly unusual scenario. From time to time, all teachers find themselves scratching their heads and thinking, "What on earth was that about?"

When I went and talked to the student in question, and to his mother, I found out some important background information. Trent's previous year of school had been horrible. He had been placed in Grade 7, but had failed almost every class in Grade 6. He was extremely anxious about the new school year, the new school, and about trying to make a clean start. He had a particular phobia about math and had barely done any at all in Grade 6, most of the time simply refusing. His academic difficulties, and more and more severe behaviour problems, seemed to exacerbate one another until he was barely functioning. Trent was suspended more than he was in school.

Trent arrived in his first math class, aware of his old classmates waiting for him to misbehave, aware of new kids who didn't know him, and aware that he was in what was for him, the most frightening class possible. Sitting with him was his self-concept, his irrational beliefs: I can't succeed at school. I am going to fail. I will never pass math. All teachers have it in for me - they all want to kick me out of school.

As soon as the teacher began to talk about evaluation and tests, Trent tapped in to those irrational beliefs and panicked. He tried to distract himself by talking to the kid next to him. The teacher, oblivious to the subtext, asked him to be quiet. Trent tapped into his beliefs about teachers and got even more agitated. He responded without thinking, fueled by his feelings, and out popped a sarcastic remark. The teacher responded more strongly and Trent was now seeing the teacher as the enemy: He has singled me out in front of everyone. I'm already in trouble in the first class. I knew this would happen and it's all this stupid teacher's fault!

By the time Trent heard that he must be quiet or leave the room, he was nearly out of control. He received the message as already being kicked out and stormed out, barely controlling his rage.

I use this example not because the conflict could have been easily avoided. On the contrary, the teacher responded normally and was blind-sided. I use it because it so clearly shows how most of the action is going on inside the kid's head - and he is not even aware of it. Even as we talked later, it was hard for Trent to see how his anxiety about school and math had contributed to his reactions. He was still sure it was the teacher's fault.

Once the teacher had some insight into Trent's background, we made a plan to deal with his anxiety and his needs around math.

Knowledge of how the conflict cycle works enables us to accept our own feelings of counter-aggression without letting them influence our behaviour. It also helps us to choose not to engage in a power struggle. I often told kids that I would not fight with them.

My knowledge of the cycle also helped me to focus my energy on the student's needs, rather than on what I was feeling.

When conflict arises, staying out of it emotionally and being able to see it and evaluate it cognitively is 90 percent of the battle. Self-talk was my greatest ally. But at the Centre I had other allies as well. It was a common strategy to switch with another adult if a conflict was starting to look like a power struggle.

One year, my colleagues in the classroom were Terry and Peter. We did a pretty good job of watching each other and if one of us was starting to argue with a kid, another would come along and ask the adult if he or she could work with another student for a bit. My intervention of choice was usually, "Junior's doing science and I don't like science. Can we switch?"

The new adult working with the upset student could decide if the problem needed to be addressed or if it was just a run-of-the-mill, "arguing is better than multiplication" situation. I remember at least one occasion, after having been totally ensnared in a power struggle, asking Peter and Terry why they didn't save me. They laughed and said they were learning by watching me "crash and burn."

Of course there were times when even using the "out" was difficult. There were times someone would provide the switch for me and it was all I could do not to say, "I don't want to switch - I'm winning!"

There were other ways to use allies. Even a word from someone else can be enough to interrupt the flow of the conflict cycle. We often just cruised by a brewing conflict and asked how things were going. That was often enough of a distraction to derail a "discussion" that looked to be heading into dangerous territory.

Over the years, I got better at using time-outs. For myself. In fact, I think my caffeine addiction peaked during my Centre years. When I felt myself getting negatively engaged with a kid, I would create breathing room by saying I needed a cup of coffee and would be right back. I got about 10 cups of coffee some days. (Don't worry - I didn't drink them all.) By the time I had walked to the kitchen and back, I was usually nice and calm and very clear about how to handle the conflict. The kid also had a little time and space to regroup, and if I went back and offered him an out, he generally took it. Sometimes I used the "coffee" defense to zip out and confer with a colleague. What did they see from their perspective? Did they have any insight

I was missing? What would they do if they were me? Could they tell me again why I was doing this job?

When I look back at it, I guess I provided kids with time-outs all the time by giving them to myself. That worked better than trying to get a kid to take a time-out. I called it a break or a change to a different activity, but it was always best received when the student saw it as something that I needed rather than something that I had decided he or she needed. Sometimes I told the student we both needed a time-out, or sometimes I told them - and I meant it - that I needed it because I was getting angry. When I returned, calm and with restored perspective, I could tell them why I had gotten angry, take responsibility for my own feelings (as I hoped they some day would take responsibility for theirs) and we could resume our discussion in a more productive direction.

When you are in the midst of a conflict, it is very difficult to manage your own emotions, decode the behaviour of the kid, and still be able to see the bigger picture at the same time. I found that I needed to visualize being outside the whole situation, seeing it in its entirety. I referred to this as "zooming out." I practised first by watching situations that I was not directly involved in or responsible for.

I remember walking into the common area one day. Both Bob and Sylvia were there, and I joined them as they stood and watched a student crawling around on the ping pong table pretending he was a cat. I immediately felt as if we should be doing something. I told myself it was not my situation to deal with and stood and observed as Bob and Sylvia watched the student with interest, even as he hurled curses at them. Afterward, I sat in the office and listened to the two of them discuss what they had observed, how it fit with this student's other behaviour patterns, what was going on at home for him right then, any changes in his academics, etc. They saw even disturbing behaviours as "just information."

Bob and Sylvia seemed to be able to see two scenarios at once: the behaviour of the child, which was like a set of armour or a cloud of dust around the kid, and the child himself, fragile and precious. They dealt with the behaviour as information and they didn't personalize it. The plans they created from what they learned were applied with compassion and caring to help the child inside that armour.

I never came close to perfecting "zooming out" - I still took things personally and got my emotions tangled up in the work. But overall, it helped me to imagine a lens pulling back to a wide angle shot. I could see the bigger picture and not focus on the little conflict at hand. And, I could remind myself that I was behind the camera, documenting, not one of the actors creating the crisis!

Sometimes, you can break the conflict cycle by calming a child before he gets really angry. Naturally, all the usual de-escalation techniques were part of my daily repertoire. Every teacher knows that when children are upset, we use a quiet and calm voice, say their name frequently, reassure them, express concern and create "team thinking" - we're in this together!

We also used humour a great deal in my classroom. With our daily report cards it was important for the adults to keep each other informed about their interactions with kids. If I didn't know about a problem at recess, I couldn't accurately fill out the report card. To this end, we got into the habit of using yellow post-it notes to put on the report card. These often became ways of de-stressing for adults - to write a quick note about an aggravating event and take some steam out of it! One day, I came to my desk and saw a note stuck to one of the report cards. It said, "Johnny can't seem to stop his goddamn swearing."

I find being ignored to be one of the tougher behaviours to deal with. It frustrates me, which is why kids do it. One day, when I felt myself getting irritated with a little boy who had been sitting like a potted plant for about 20 minutes, I decided to try a new approach. I don't actually recommend this, but it worked well when I picked him up and threw him over my shoulder and started to leave the Centre, telling Bob that I was taking Jeffrey to the hospital because he had gone stone deaf. I ranted all the way to the door, and by then Jeffrey was giggling and we all had a laugh. It's really hard to go back into a stonewall temper tantrum after you've just had a good belly laugh.

Usually, when someone chose to ignore me, I used one standard line. I would turn to whoever was nearby, student or staff, and say quickly, "Can you hear me? Can you see me? Am I still here?" They would laugh, I would laugh. The student in pouting mode may or may not have responded, but I would not feel frustrated any more and I was okay to let them be.

One year I went to Phoenix for the winter break. I had never been on a warm winter holiday before and I was excited. I had told the kids about my excitement and used it in a "teachable moment" one day as we discussed things we all can do to focus our thoughts positively so we don't feel anxious or angry. I told them that when I was feeling frustrated in the classroom, I was making myself think about Phoenix. Each of the kids had their own ideas and I remember it was a particularly funny discussion. A few days later, a student was getting quite argumentative and aggressive with me in the middle of class time. I was sitting at my desk, trying to derail him and was starting to feel some counter-aggression bubbling. All the kids were tuned in, so I said to one of the spectators, "David, quick, I'm losing it. Help me!"

David jumped to his feet and yelled, "Phoenix. Phoenix! Think about Phoenix!"

One last thing about conflict. Keep in mind that most of the conflicts that arise in the classroom are not really about the incident at hand. This makes it easier to depersonalize. When a student tells you your map lesson sucks, it could be that your map lesson sucks. More likely, the student has a really hard time understanding maps. Or the student has never had a map lesson before and is afraid of new things. Or perhaps she is mad at you about something from two days ago that you are oblivious to. Or maybe she is mad at someone else in the class. Or someone at home. Perhaps she's not angry at all. Maybe she is feeling tired, or afraid, or ashamed, or worried, or even excited. My point is that difficult kids don't portray their feelings accurately, let alone understand them or handle them appropriately. The challenge is to stay zoomed out and find out what the underlying issue is.

As I write, and I think about this specific process of unraveling these little mysteries, I can think of many, many incidents that began with some little inappropriate behaviour and ended up leading to great talks about big issues.

It is a difficult and sometimes painful process to teach oneself to get comfortable with conflict. Looking back, I see how that process alone altered my teaching. Instead of seeing conflict as an undesirable detour, it became one of the best parts of teaching because it produced the best kinds of learning.

I became a teacher because I love kids, not geography. When I worked through conflicts with kids, I had an opportunity to teach them all the very best things about being human: compassion, forgiveness, connectedness, growth, self awareness, and understanding others. Frankly, someone else can teach them geography.

4. Long & Wood, 1991. (pp. 36,37)
5. Long & Wood, 1991. (pp. 33-34, 46-49)

Chapter 6

Communication

Listening is harder than it sounds

istening is one of the most fundamental tools for working with at-risk kids. Perhaps it is the fundamental tool for many things. I never gave much thought to my listening skills pre-Centre. I didn't interrupt and I understood what I was told most of the time. I figured that made me a good listener.

Then I started listening to kids at the Centre. Over the years I listened to coded messages, nonsensical streams of ideas, and extravagantly embellished stories. I listened to kids tell me that nothing was wrong, they were perfectly fine, nothing to worry about, as they lay in the fetal position on a desk, or hid behind a "fort" of couch cushions. I usually had absolutely no idea what they were trying to tell me.

Because words are such a small percentage of the message, I left that to last. I began with trying to decode body language. I found that difficult. I was good at being able to figure out what kids were feeling - that was a gift of instinct, largely. But I had a surprisingly difficult time with decoding specific messages because I didn't read body language well. (I never did and still don't - I'm the type who leaves a meeting and has to ask someone else how it went because I just don't pick up on all the subtext and body language.)

When I met with kids I knew how they felt, but had no idea why. Often my boss would seem surprised that I was still wondering what was creating their feelings and would point out the clues I had missed: the increased restlessness of hands when a certain topic arose, change in eye contact, change in voice volume and/or tone, change in body position or posture. There were many ways to "read" kids, and learning those things took time for me. The challenge was always in trying to stay fully present with the child in my listening, while letting part of my brain attend to the non-verbal cues. I found it helpful to videotape conversations and look for clues later.

My strongest example happened the day I asked the children's counsellor from the Addictions Foundation of Manitoba to have an introductory meeting with the kids, just to get to know them and let them get comfortable with her. I was suspicious that one little guy was living with an alcoholic, and wanted to be able to access the counsellor for him if necessary. The kids were used to the video camera as I was taping in the classroom a lot with that group (with parental permission, of course).

The boy's behaviour quickly deteriorated to a major meltdown and ended in a restraint situation. I was discouraged, feeling that the counsellor's time had been wasted and I would have to start again to build some rapport between her and my student. However, when I watched the tape, I realized how true it is that "everything is information."

This student had a large repertoire of bizarre behaviours that surfaced in times of stress. One was to pretend he was a cat. We came to understand that this was an indication of extreme feelings of vulnerability. As I watched the tape, I noted that Alex was acting like a cat right from the start. That was unusual, as he usually worked himself up to that level. He was sitting at the table listening politely with the rest of the group one minute, the next minute he slid off his chair and crouched under the table "meowing." I went back and increased the volume. The counsellor was introducing herself and learning their names and chatting away. Alex was relaxed and participating. At the precise moment that she used the word "alcohol" for the first time, he slid off his chair and became a cat. Information.

They weren't all that brick-on-the-head obvious, but there were many times when a change in behaviour, or even posture, could provide us with valuable information.

Obviously, all children have their own language. They each have their own "tell" - a little behaviour that gives them away when they are feeling stress. For some kids, their walk changes. Many decrease eye contact. Some become restless, moving and fidgeting constantly. Some students rub their heads, others tap with their fingers or whatever is in their hand at the moment, some chew lips or crack knuckles, or get the "jimmy legs" - bouncing a knee up and down rapidly while sitting. There were certain scowls and even certain smiles that were warnings that something was up. These parts of our Early

Warning Detection System were easy enough to spot once you got to know the students. What I found more challenging was decoding their behaviour while they were actually trying to tell you something specific, but didn't know how.

This decoding took a lot of practice and attention. Being attentive to each student in normal and especially happy situations, noting body language at those times, made it a bit easier to read them in more difficult circumstances.

When we were talking privately, I would note a change in posture and I would stop them and ask the students what they were feeling. Some kids could articulate that they suddenly felt happy or angry or sad. If they didn't know, I would ask them where they felt something and they would describe the physical expressions of their feelings in their bodies. Together we could figure out what they were feeling and how that connected to what we were talking about. Once I became conversant in a student's body language, I could decode for myself as we talked.

I would say that the majority of the kids I worked with gave away more information through their bodies than through tone or words. However, I began to work on listening to tone more. I practised this with kids who hid their faces while they talked. Since they were not looking at me, I could close my eyes and listen to them. For some reason, I found it easier to hear changes in tone this way.

Many kids have been conditioned to always say "the right thing." This is a bit of a rarity amongst at-risk kids, but there were a few. They continued to speak appropriate words as their bodies and voices gave a different message. At some point they would likely lose their control. Getting familiar with tone and body language helped circumnavigate many minor crises ahead of the explosion. In time, I could listen to my group playing a table game in another room and monitor the situation without being able to see the kids or hear the words. The tone of each voice kept me up to speed.

With words it is important to attend to each one of them. When I watch talk shows on television and hear cryptic little comments dropped out of context by guests, I always want the host to ask about the comment, dig a little and find out where it came from. They rarely do. It's annoying.

When kids dropped little items that didn't fit into their stories, I wanted to go after those tidbits. If the entire story had been one long "whopper" about what they did on the weekend and then there was suddenly a mundane little detail, that is where I started. Often, it was not a whole sentence, just a phrase or a word shoved into a conversation like a wedge. I visualized those wedges as doorstops, and knew that if I were quick enough, and tread very gently, I might be allowed through an important door before it closed again.

One day, one of my all-time favourite students was in an especially cranky mood. His walk, or rather, his stomp across the common area caught my eye. I followed him into the classroom to say good morning and received a grunt in reply. He shouldered past me and sat at his desk and put his head down. I tried to talk with him but was told clearly (and quite colourfully) that he wished to be left alone. We gave him lots of space during the first half of the morning and he kept to himself, working through his task list on his own.

Gradually, he began to get a bit more interactive and joined the group for our science lesson. He was quiet and pale and I was concerned. After science, he seemed a bit more like himself and I invited him for a visit in the meeting room. He came willingly and sat on the couch staring at me warily. I asked him if he was hungry or tired. He said no. I told him he looked as if he had "lots of feelings going on." He nodded and suddenly looked very sad. I asked if he knew what his feelings were about, and he said that he didn't. I took a few guesses based on previous discussions and he brushed them all aside angrily. He grew impatient with me abruptly, as if he had changed his mind about wanting to be there at all. He told me he was going back to the #*!%@!! classroom to finish his work.

As Darren was basically a non-reader, I knew that he had completed all the work on his list that he could do independently. I asked if he would like to work in the meeting room with me. I was needing a quiet place to work and if I had a kid with me, that would make it look better! Always willing to be my co-conspirator, Darren agreed to help and shuffled off with his cute "little old man" walk to get his stuff.

We sat and worked for about half an hour, chatting amiably as we went. I finally felt he was calm and relaxed and asked the question I suspected would trigger him either to talk or blow up: I asked how his weekend had been. He looked at me for a second and I watched clouds of emotion race across his face.

"I hate that fucking truck!" he yelled.

I asked what truck he was talking about and got a full ten minutes of loud, colourful, and angry narration about riding in the family truck all the way to Saskatchewan with too many people. He was mad at everyone in the truck and spent another 10 minutes or so berating everyone for everything they had done to bug him in the past several weeks. That led to his usual tirade about his regular issues and he took another five minutes or so to finally run out of steam. He finished with another declaration of hatred for the truck, trailed off lamely and sat looking exhausted.

"Where did you drive to in the truck, Darren?"

"To my uncle's funeral," he said.

As I write, I try to remember a single Darren story that didn't create a blue cloud of curse words. I can't remember any. Back in the days when I was offended by such language, I probably killed a lot of important stories in the early stages by expressing my discomfort with the language in some way. Darren and I had zillions of opportunities to discuss word choices, but I believe we may have only had one chance to talk about losing his uncle.

On another occasion, a boy we'll call Bruce, about nine years old, came into school one morning in an especially "up" mood. He was at times bouncy, loud and goofy, and then sad. He laughed at everything and found himself especially hysterical. He seemed a little manic to me, and I watched him closely. From time to time he would repeat a nonsensical word and then laugh uproariously. The roller coaster went up and down; he vacillated between silly and sullen all morning. At lunchtime, as we sat in the kitchen eating, he said his word again and belted out his laugh, which was starting to sound a bit strained. I kept a close eye on him during lunch break and then asked him to come for a "visit" when it was time to go back to the classroom.

We chatted for a while and then I mentioned how much fun he appeared to be having that morning. I asked him about his word and he grew quiet and looked at me for a while as if he were deciding whether to feed me a line or tell me the truth. What he told me next certainly sounded like a line, but I believe it was his truth. He became deadly serious, his big, brown eyes looking huge and frightened.

He told me the word was the name of a man. He described the man as being very tall and dark and shadowy. He could never see him completely. His confused description and his explanation of where and when he had seen the man got me wondering if this might be a nightmare scene. I asked how he knew the man's name and he said he "just knew." He talked for a long time about his fear of the man, and while the actual events he was describing were obviously from his imagination, the fear was very real.

It was clear to me as I listened that he had been desperately needing to get the two of us talking about his "fear man," and yet the only way he had known to get a message to me was shouting out that name and laughing.

As an aside, Bruce's shadow man became a regular player in our talks. He was Bruce's way of embodying all the elusive, unidentifiable fears that surrounded him as he lived with his recovering alcoholic mother and woke up each morning bathed in a feeling of uncertainty. What the shadow man had been up to the night before was information for me about how things were at Bruce's house. Eventually, we named some of those fears and sent the shadow man on his way. I always used Bruce's vivid imagination to my advantage in discussions with him and I never forgot to check out new words that materialized in my classroom.

There are probably countless stories of listening buried in my memory. My overall feeling as I look back and think of all those hours I spent with kids, listening to them, being with them in their stories, is a feeling of gratitude. It is the most humbling honour to be allowed inside the landscape of another person's heart. I am amazed at the courage of those children who opened that door and allowed me to step inside with all their secrets and fears and vulnerabilities. I pray my footsteps were light. I pray for that same kind of courage.

Chapter 7

Kids and Anger

The tip of the iceberg

Helping children learn to deal with anger in an educational setting is very much like trying to help them negotiate around an iceberg. Children can see the tip, the explosion or outward manifestation of their feelings of anger. They believe, and are sometimes told, that just steering around that tip is the solution. They are told to "count to ten," or "go for a walk", or "hit a pillow." None of these are bad ideas, but they only address symptom relief. They do not address the problem. Some kids do manage to control their outbursts with these and other strategies, and while they may be avoiding the big, visible collisions, they are likely grinding constantly against the problem below the surface. That can cause irreparable damage to a child without anyone noticing.

Knowing that there is always more below the surface is important. As classroom teachers, we may not have the opportunity to explore below the surface with the student, but someone must. Counselling, talking, problem-solving - call it what you like - children who have difficulty controlling anger will eventually have to examine what lies below the tip of the iceberg. The earlier they learn how to deal with the root causes of their anger, the more positive their life can be.

There are exceptions. There are kids who become irrational and aggressive for physiological reasons such as food allergies, low blood sugar, petit mal seizures, and other chemical-body reasons. A child with violent or aggressive behaviour should always be seen by a physician first to rule out all the physical possibilities.

Many times, the apparent reason for behaviour problems in the classroom is academic difficulty. This is very real and in my experience, frequent. However, addressing academics is not enough. By the time a child is acting out, he or she has likely been struggling with the content for a long time. The erosion of self-esteem, the feelings of alienation from teachers and peers, family tension and disruption, have added many layers to the child's distress.

In addition, any number of irrational beliefs may have developed within many kids to help them cope with what they are experiencing in the classroom.

Kids create patterns of behaviour to avoid the most threatening or painful experiences. Again, almost all kids choose to look bad over looking stupid. There was a girl at the Centre who displayed a lot of anger. Over time, staff noticed a pattern in the endless stream of crises created by Josie. Every day there was either a new "problem" that Josie needed to discuss with the director immediately, or an explosion or outburst of some kind. At 10:00 a.m.

Once staff recognized the pattern and connected that 10:00 a.m. was time for math, the real problem could be addressed. While her math lessons could be adapted easily enough, and while staff knew how to help Josie with her fear of math, helping her stop the pattern of avoidance whenever she felt discomfort was a more involved process of problem-solving. Slowly, she was able to acknowledge the pattern, see the negative effects of it, and begin to explore new ways of handling her math phobia.

I remember another teenager who seemed to be angry all the time. Most days, he stomped around so that everyone around him gave him a wide berth. There were regular blow-ups about ridiculous little things: someone "giving him a look," someone touching his things, or whatever he could point to as a reason for his anger. The explosion would be loud and colourful, but it lacked substance. After having Ben at the Centre for several weeks, it became obvious that the outbursts and all the simmering anger were his protection. He created an effective barrier around himself with all his huffing and puffing, a buffer zone that kept everyone in his life at a safe and manageable distance. Ben was actually scared - really scared! His choice for managing his constant fear was to create a little space for himself. A lonely, but effective management tool.

With Ben, it was important to make relationship a priority. The cure for fear is trust and eventually, when all his tempest of behaviour did not push the adults at the Centre out of his life, he began to relax a little. More time, more trust, more connection, less commotion. The process of talking and learning could begin.

Another student, a 12-year-old girl with a severe hearing loss and a history of abuse and neglect, became increasingly violent as she got older. It was heartbreaking to watch Tammy, a child with a positive and friendly nature, become angrier and angrier. Her frustration with her hearing loss and the miscommunications that constantly arose led to more and more violence. The affection and compassion of caring foster parents was never enough to make her feel loved. How angry and desperate does a child have to be to swallow her own hearing aid? Because this child lacked a home she connected to, all our efforts as educators were secondary. We tried to provide a place where she felt safe and accepted. She was provided with a very skilled TA, fluent in American Sign Language, and given as much support and caring as possible. Sadly, it eventually became unsafe to have her at the Centre.

There were kids who lashed out in anger whenever they felt any danger, real or perceived. Their abusive pasts created oversensitivity and distrust and they were easily triggered into lashing out to stay safe - I will hurt or reject you before you can hurt or reject me. The adult is safely pushed away and the child carries on in the belief that he or she is alone and adults are not to be trusted. This behaviour reflects beliefs. It requires compassion and acceptance to keep relationships viable in spite of sometimes abusive behaviour. When the usual repertoire of tricks didn't alienate the staff, when problems were discussed instead of merely punished, hurt kids could begin to trust again. As with Ben, spending less time keeping everyone scared off allowed these students to engage with us in looking at their ineffective patterns of behaviour and creating motivation for change.

I met kids who saw their anger as their only strength. It protected them and brought them status. Their perception was that others "made" them angry and they had a responsibility to "deal with it." Their fighting prowess brought them respect from their peers. I think of two non-reader teenage boys who both considered their fighting skills to be their only asset. These kids needed to hear, from adults they had learned they could trust, that they had other strengths.

There were kids who insisted they never got mad. There were no huge, out-of-control outbursts, but the simmering was always there. These were often the kids who "kept score" and were masterful at orchestrating elaborate revenges for perceived wrongs. This was misdirected anger a lot of the time, held back from a parent or some situation that they felt they did not have a right to be angry about. After the fact, they could rationalize their behaviour. Finding out about past or present circumstances and allowing kids - encouraging kids - to express their anger appropriately, was a big first step.

Over seven years I obviously met a lot of angry kids. To discover the nature of their anger and where it came from brought me patience and compassion. It gave me direction in helping them go below the surface and explore the iceberg. But before finding that understanding, it was necessary to address the anger itself.

Many kids came to us knowing their anger was a problem, and wanting help. They understood that issues involving their anger were constantly creating negative events in their lives. For many of them, this was the reason they found themselves in a new school. Others felt justified in their anger and in their violence. Usually, they attributed their anger to the wrong things: the actions of others, or surface events. My first job was to get a student on board with wanting to "look at the anger thing."

Some kids I could persuade to start a dialogue by pointing out that anger and violence were bringing them all kinds of consequences that they did not like, regardless of whether they felt their actions were justified or not. Sometimes I could start by selling them "symptom relief" (how can I get that principal off my ass?), and move to examining the appropriateness of their behaviour at a later date.

Jeremy was an 8-year-old boy who found it difficult to communicate. When he did try to reach out to the only other person in his household, his mother, he was given the message that he really shouldn't be burdening her with his troubles and needed to learn to handle them on his own. He struggled through the frustration of being a weak student in a classroom that felt overwhelming for him. Eventually, he would blow. When he came to us at the Centre, we saw the same pattern. He tried to hold it together, kept smiling and saying that things were okay. I would point out situations I'd observed and tell him that if I were in his shoes, I would be frustrated or upset. He would insist that it hadn't bothered him and on we would go until the inevitable explosion.

Soon, I began to "diagram" this pattern for him. My sad stickman sketches were enough to help him see that many days looked the same, with their pattern of minor upsets that he refused to acknowledge, and the final "blow."

One day, I invited Jeremy into the Quiet Room for a visit. I brought a balloon with me and asked if I could tell him about a couple of days from my week.

On the first day, I went to the swimming pool in the morning and it was closed. That made me feel upset. I blew a bit of air into the balloon. On the way to work, my car heater wasn't working properly and by the time I got to work, I felt cold and cranky. I blew a bit more air into the balloon. As soon as I arrived, my boss wanted to speak to me about something I had forgotten to do. I felt embarrassed and guilty. I blew more air into the balloon. When the kids arrived from the bus, they were arguing and being rude. (I blew a bit of air into the balloon), and when I tried to help them sort out their conflict, one of them told me to shut up. That made me feel mad. More air into the balloon. At noon, I had a meeting that went so long I didn't have time to eat. I felt hungry and cranky. More air. On the story went, until the balloon was almost bursting. I asked Jeremy what was going to happen if I blew any more "feelings" into that poor balloon.

"It will explode," he responded confidently. We talked about what that might look like in the context of me and my bad day. I let the air out of the balloon and then I told him the story of another day.

My alarm didn't go off and I had to rush off without breakfast or a shower or going for a swim. I blew lots of air into the balloon. When I got to work, Terry asked me how I was and I told her about my crazy morning and how frustrated it made me feel. I let the air out of the balloon. I had to do someone else's bus duty and it was freezing cold and snowing. I blew air into the balloon. When I came back in, I told Bob how cold it was and how I don't like bus duty and Bob made a joke about how I always complain about bus duty and we both laughed because that's true. I let the air out of the balloon. So went the story of the second day: air in, air out. Feelings in, feelings out. At the end of the tale of the second day, Jeremy took the empty balloon from me and said, "My mom was really crabby to me this morning." And we talked about it. Feelings out.

I tried to keep a supply of balloons on hand at all times.

With older kids, I borrowed a page from Rational Emotive

Behaviour Therapy.[6] (My own version of course.) I usually used this early in a relationship, when I knew they liked and trusted me, but before we had done a lot of tough work in our counselling or talking. In a general conversation about anger, I would ask if they had been given tips about managing anger before. They all recited the same tired list for me. I would ask if counting to 100 or any of the other methods worked for them and got answers ranging from "sometimes" to "never." I would nod knowingly and give my "that's interesting" grunt. Eventually they could get it out of me that I was in possession of the REAL secret to handling anger and if they were interested, I might tell them about it sometime. "Sometime" was usually fairly soon.

Once I had them hooked, we talked about the difference between anger and violent behaviour. It was stunning how many kids did not differentiate. Breaking a window was to them "being angry." Getting them to differentiate between the feeling and the behaviour sometimes took a while. It took even longer to get comfortable with accepting the term "violence" to mean any behaviour that had a hurtful impact on others. Whether we settled on "violence" or "aggressive behaviour" for terminology, the point was to be sure kids saw a difference between the feeling of anger and the behaviours or acts that were associated with that anger.

I asked them to tell me what caused them to be violent. Without fail, they recited the incidents that they saw as having created their violent reactions: when he pushed me, when she stole from me, when they laughed at me, etc. I would write down the word "incident" and draw an arrow from it to the word "behaviour." They would confirm for me that this was their theory of how their aggressive behaviour worked: the initial incident caused the aggressive behaviour. I would then propose a story to test their theory:

Imagine you are walking down the street. A person walking toward you bangs into your shoulder pretty heavily as they pass by. What will you do?

Most kids relished the opportunity to tell me in gruesome detail what they would do to "get that guy back."

How do you feel?

Angry, they all replied.

Now imagine that same scene again: you are walking along, minding your own business, when someone bangs into your shoulder. You turn around to look and notice the person is walking with a white cane. How do you feel now?

Now the kids thought they would not be angry because they knew the person was blind and did not do it on purpose.

Yes, but the original incident did not change. In both instances, someone banged into your shoulder really hard. Once you got angry and once you did not. What is the difference?

They had a million answers.

What is missing in your theory?

They usually came up with "feelings."

Excellent. Now we are getting somewhere. Where do feelings fit in your equation?

The kids realized that the incident caused feelings and the feelings caused the behaviour. We amended the diagram. We discussed the probability of the same incident creating the same feelings.

Hmm. But in our blind walker incident, we had the same incident with two different feelings. Something is missing.

At this point I would add a mystery box to the diagram. It went right after the incident box. I would heartily agree that our feelings create our reactions.

But what creates the feelings? If it was just the incident, we would have been mad both times we got bumped. What happened between the incident and the feeling in the second scenario?

I suggested that we noticed the person was blind. We THOUGHT to ourselves that it was an accident. No angry feelings. The mystery box was our thoughts—what we say to ourselves about what happens to us.

We discussed what self-talk may have been going on in the first scenario: "That's not fair," "They have no right," "I don't have to put up with that." Messages that create anger in us.

I believe it is important for kids to understand this concept and to begin to practise listening to their own internal tape. With kids who really "got it" and wanted to work with it, we discussed the types of language that can create frustration or anger: words like "always" and "never" are indicators that global thinking is going on, and while not getting picked for soccer can be upsetting, thinking, "I never get picked for soccer" creates far stronger feelings. I have challenged kids to listen to what is happening in their heads from time to time during the day and see if they catch themselves thinking thoughts that incite them.

If they can do this, they can use self-talk to their advantage. They can learn to give themselves messages that divert feelings of anger before they are created. This is a skill that takes a lot of practice (don't I know!) but kids can start learning it. Some will cut down on their incidents because they simply stopped to think! Some will be advanced enough to begin to change the internal messages that create negative feelings all the time. Others will realize that they are participants in the events of their lives, not hapless victims with no responsibility for their actions. Others will be introduced to the idea that there is something going on inside their heads and perhaps they will revisit the idea somewhere further down the road in their lives.

With young kids, I have introduced this idea with the story of someone bursting into my classroom and telling one of the kids and myself that we have been chosen to go to Disneyland for a week. I ask the student what they are going to do and they usually say they are going home to pack. I tell them I am going to the kitchen for a cup of coffee because I feel upset. Same incident, different reactions. We both got the same news, but our different feelings created different reactions. What caused such different feelings? Different thoughts:

Yahoo! No school for a week. Rides and games and fun and a plane ride and a hotel. When do we leave?

Oh no! A week. I hate airplanes and rides. It is going to be so hot and crowded, and I'll miss my family so much. Who wants to go somewhere with millions of kids? Do I have to go?

The process is different with younger kids but the point is the same. If we tell ourselves things are unfair or people are out to get us or nothing good ever happens to us, we create negative feelings that can lead us to make negative choices in our behaviour. With little kids I wanted to plant the seeds of awareness and responsibility. "Stop and think" was such a popular mantra for a while, that we made our own stop sign to cue the kids. A word of warning: poorly timed use of the stop sign can be hazardous to the stop sign's health. Rest in peace, stop sign.

I spent seven years of my professional life struggling every day to find ways to help kids get a handle on their anger - help them learn to understand it and to manage it, and hopefully, to gain independence from it in the end. I tried anything I could think of. I told a thousand stories meant to soothe, to encourage, to teach. I made jokes at the right time and sometimes at the wrong time. I learned the hard way about some kids' anger. I invented angry puppet characters and learned to love them along with the kids. I rubbed backs and held hands and dried angry tears, and tried to believe myself when I told them it was going to be okay.

I went into angry places with kids and sat there shaking while we looked around together and tried to figure out exactly where we were and if there was an easier way to get out than the one we used to get in. I learned to see anger as all the different things that it was: a tool, a bartering chip, a distraction, protection, camouflage, fear, pain.

I learned that anger looks different in every person, that it serves a purpose, that it is not a bad thing. As I learned to be comfortable with the anger of kids, I could give myself permission to feel angry. I learned that every time I told a little one he had a right to his feelings of anger, I was finally hearing it for myself. I learned to stop fearing my own anger.

It has taken time for some of the lessons of the Centre to become clear for me. This is one that is ongoing. I imagine a time when I will be as comfortable with anger - mine or that of others - as I am with joy. I continue to look for the lessons of anger and the gifts of the learning.

6. REBT is the therapy developed by Albert Ellis. It is based on the concept that our thoughts create or help to create our feelings. How we interpret events in our lives, determines our feelings about them.

Chapter 8

The Bottom Line
Re-examining boundaries

We all have to maintain personal boundaries to make sure that we care for ourselves. Normally, this is not an issue in most relationships. You have a general sense of when someone comes close to that boundary and you may feel more wary and watchful, but in healthy relationships, we are rarely called upon to define that boundary, let alone defend it. Working with children in today's schools means most teachers must define that boundary for themselves. At what point will we go to our administrator and say, "I can't be in the classroom right now." Is it when someone tells us to fuck off? Is it when a student throws a book at us? Is it when a student threatens us with violence? Do we even feel we have the right to make that stand?

When I graduated from university, I thought I knew exactly where that line was. Then I had a student I really liked tell me to fuck off. I knew what was going on in her personal life. I held her accountable for how she handled the situation, but I also looked very closely at how I handled it. Knowing her situation, I could have been more flexible with my expectations of her right then. Perhaps we could have avoided the blow-up that way. I found that I was not the least bit interested in her being "punished" for telling me off. My boundary became a bit fuzzy.

The years went on and I dealt with more and more "unacceptable" behaviour from kids who were dealing with unacceptable situations in their personal lives. My boundary faded, moved and returned, got trampled and squashed, and was all but forgotten. Without much conscious consideration, my boundary settled at the point of my physical safety. I felt physically threatened a couple of times but no one ever really tried to hurt me.

When I got to the Centre, they really tried to hurt me!

I jest. No one wanted to hurt me, but there were lots of violent kids and suddenly my boundary had to be re-examined.

In the introduction to this book, I talked about trying to explain to a non-teacher why we "put up with abusive behaviour." This is what I am talking about now. To sit over a cup of coffee and discuss what is acceptable and unacceptable behaviour for a teacher is not realistic. In that conversation a few years back, I would have told you that I would never accept kids calling me names. But I remember a day when I was called every name in the book by a little boy who had been treated horribly the night before by his mother. The boy told me what was going on at home. I had had no choice but to call the child protection authorities. I don't recall wondering about my personal boundaries as I listened to his sobbing rant about me betraying him. I do remember thinking he may have been right.

We are put in positions all the time where black and white becomes grey in a big hurry.

I don't accept kids hitting. One day, a little boy in a rage caused by hurt and rejection, threw whatever he could get his hands on at whomever he saw. We had to restrain him. When he finally calmed down and I let him go, the little 65 pounds of him turned and took a swipe at me, because I had just held him in restraint for ten long minutes. Of course he did - I would have, too.

Another extremely violent young man had to be restrained quickly one day, and there was no time to think. We held him to the ground and I ended up with my arm crossing his body to hold his arm. He latched onto my forearm with his teeth. He was being pinned to the ground, emotions out of control, and there was an arm within range - an opportunity for him to feel some control or self-protection. I wore long sleeves for weeks so none of us would have to be reminded of that ugly incident of which the bite was just one small part.

I have heard teachers use the phrase, "I don't have to put up with that." I often wonder what feeling goes with that. They usually sound angry, but I wonder if there isn't fear there too. It is scary to have to re-examine boundaries. It is scary to think that the nice thick wall that keeps us safely separated from the kids we work with might not be so thick after all. When we decide over coffee what is black and what is white, what is acceptable and what is unacceptable, what we can handle and what we will "not put up with," we leave ourselves with little room for compassion. Walls don't just protect us, they keep us from any depth in our relationships. If you have a preconceived notion about what "must be punished, regardless of the circumstances," you will open yourself to two dangers.

First, you will have to devote a lot of your emotional energy to being vigilant about your boundaries. When they are breeched, you will feel offended and will spend a lot of energy on managing your own feelings of outrage and hurt. Being watchful of a boundary keeps your eyes more on the boundary and on yourself than on the people around you.

The second danger is that when you are really angry, when you have been pushed beyond the beyond, your unconscious mind will remind you that there is a boundary. It may even remind you that if the child steps over that boundary, they will be punished. I have witnessed many incidents where I could not explain the actions of the adult involved in any other way than that they were trying to push the student over that boundary. I recall many times watching adults follow kids who were trying to escape the blow-up. I think of a teacher - a competent, caring teacher - who was past his limit and was relentless with a student, even barring the door as the student tried to leave. When the student finally pushed the teacher in an effort to get out the door, she was suspended from school. Perhaps, unconsciously, that was the desired outcome for the teacher. I have wondered about my own motivation when I have been involved in a power struggle that ended with the student "crossing the line" and being suspended.

The first time I was hurt by a student, I remember feeling a bit outraged. I knew that my boundary had been offended and I wanted justice! I went home and thought about whether the Centre was the right place for me. Was I subjecting myself to something I shouldn't? Was I being respectful of my personal boundaries to work in such an atmosphere?

I decided that it would all depend on how the matter was resolved. I spoke with my bosses the next morning about how to handle it. We immediately began talking about how the student was likely to be feeling when he came to school and how we could make that better for him. We talked about what would be most comfortable for the student, how to approach him, who should talk to him, how best to involve his parent. The discussion went on and on and I grew quieter and quieter.

I knew the process. This was the first time I had received a well-landed punch, but by no means the first incident of aggression towards me. I somehow thought that this would be different but it seemed to me that Bob and Sylvia saw it as just another incident to be problem-solved. They inquired about my withdrawal from the discussion and I told them some lie. How could I tell them what I felt? Hey. This isn't fair. That kid hurt me and no one cares about me! Aren't you going to suspend him, throw the book at him? I want justice!

Sylvia listened to my dishonest reply and asked, "Are you wanting to resolve this or are you wanting revenge?" Her eyes were twinkling and I felt no recrimination from her, but an instant shame in myself. I was the adult. A little child had lost control of his already fragile emotions and lashed out at me in fear. He was probably ashamed, afraid to come to school, afraid he had ruined a relationship that I knew he valued, and feeling disappointment that he had "blown it again." I had to find a way to put my needs aside and focus on his. It wasn't that my needs weren't valued at the Centre - they were. But I needed to accept exactly why I was there.

I would like to report that I was the picture of compassion and grace when that student arrived to problem solve. That would be a fib. I tried to focus on the student, but as soon as I saw him, my own emotional response took a lot of my attention. I did the best I could, relied heavily on Bob during the session, and felt a little distant from that student for a while.

It got easier and easier to handle situations that crossed my boundaries, particularly when I could see the response of the kids. Instead of being rejected again (suspended), they were allowed and expected to talk about what had happened. They could try to make amends. They got another chance and were not treated like outcasts because they screwed up. And they had to hear from the person they hurt. We all know from experience how hard it is to listen while someone you care about describes how it feels to be hurt by you.

Most of all, I could see results. Many kids only hit once at the Centre. In the past, punishment without discussion might have fueled their feelings of persecution and justified their violence in their minds. Having to talk about it was different. Having to work through it with the other person was very different. The real power was in still having the support and nurturing of the person you offended after it was all over and done with - the incident, the problem-solving, and the consequences. This is the very heart of learning: to be with a child in the midst of a crisis, even as the "injured" party, and help her see what is happening, and guide her to learn and change.

Many times over the years, Sylvia asked, "Are you looking for revenge?" Many times I responded with a hearty, "Yes, I am!" That was my gentle reminder that it wasn't about me. It was about that hurting child who needed my help, my support, my guidance and definitely not my vengeance.

This lesson has come to life in many areas of my consciousness. I am not talking about accepting or condoning violence. I am simply saying that if punishment isn't working, maybe compassion can.

As I have learned to see the whole picture with violent kids, I have thought a lot about violent adults. Why is a violent 14-year-old seen as a victim in need of our help, and an 18-year-old seen as an enemy of society who should be locked up forever? Why do we hit kids in order to teach them not to hit?

Everyone has to determine his own bottom line. Here's mine: every situation is unique, every child is unique, I am unique. In each circumstance I will look at how those three elements have come together and decide on a "bottom line" that makes both me and the child feel safe and challenged to grow.

Chapter 9

Hitting the Wall

Can they trust `new guy´?

After a student had been with us for a little while, he would often regress into a period of negative behaviour. It typically came around the time that staff members were patting each other on the back and saying, "I think Junior might be ready to try a day at his home school." Then all hell would break loose. There are lots of reasons this might happen, but my personal theory was that some of the kids just hit the wall.

They had come a long way, worked hard, and made changes. They came to where they could manage their lives and emotions and therefore, behaviour, in a consistently positive manner. As soon as they realized this, they'd freak. For the students, hitting the wall was the final hurdle to jump. It meant looking in the mirror and seeing someone they could live with. When they didn't find the old, familiar, predictable, dysfunctional self, they panicked. They couldn't identify with the new person and they didn't know them. They certainly didn't trust the "new guy" to handle the tests that they knew were coming: family, school, peer issues. The old kid, miserable as he may have been, had found a way to survive. The thought of taking "new guy" into the real world was terrifying for many kids. The wall was the collision between the relative safety and security of the Centre, and who they were in that context, and who they were or thought they needed to be in the rest of their world. Many times we witnessed self-destruction.

Most kids really liked the feel of being "on track." You could watch them blossom as they began to deal with their issues and make changes. The big tests were in times of duress. As we began to transition them back to their home schools, there were always times of regression. When something went wrong and the stress level went up, most kids snapped back to their old behaviours. Again, they just didn't trust "new guy" to get them through it. We would problem-solve and they usually knew exactly how they should have handled it. We had to help them visualize themselves using their new skills in the "old" context, applying their new knowledge and methods to the same old problems. We had to help them visualize a positive outcome for letting "new guy" handle the problem. We were coaches and cheerleaders, but we could do nothing but watch as those brave little kids went back to their old schools and tried to be new people.

Most classroom teachers did a great job of helping with the transition. They made a point of learning the same skills the child had acquired - problem-solving, etc. Some teachers even helped prepare their class for the return of the student so he or she would have a fighting chance. Many teachers made a point of staying connected with their student the whole time they were with us, coming to spend a half-day with them, learning how things worked at the Centre, and trying to find out the best way to help their student make the transition back successfully.

One of my favourite memories is this: A teacher and counsellor were visiting a little girl from their school (which was the furthest away geographically but did a great job of staying connected to their students). I looked through the window into the office during their visit and all three were squished together on the tiny couch, little one in the middle. Both adults were totally focused on her, totally "with" her, as she chatted away happily, head swiveling back and forth between them, with a huge smile on her face.

I guess I love that memory so much because it helps make up for all the times we dealt with teachers who were not able or willing to give much to returning students. It was heartbreaking to watch a student go back to school, try and try, and eventually give up because no one would acknowledge or validate the changes they had made. Often, when there is dysfunction in a classroom, it is easy for us as adults to put the blame on "the troublemaker" and abdicate ourselves of any responsibility.

When you send "new guy" back to that atmosphere and nothing has changed there, when everyone around him is waiting for him to mess up, when the adults who are supposed to be helping still treat him with suspicion and even hostility, I can guarantee that school will get exactly what they predicted.

I like to think that even with kids who appeared to regress completely, that they had time to build some kind of attachment to their "new guy." Perhaps, someday, they will remember the self they uncovered at the Centre. I like to think they will remember the self they saw in the mirror - remember how it felt, and remember how others responded to them. I like to think that those positive memories will be enough to send them on another journey to find that self again.

Interestingly, the adults who worked at the Centre experienced our own version of hitting the wall.

One day, a colleague approached me as I sat working at my desk after school.

"Do you have a minute?" she asked. She proceeded to tell me a story about her personal life, how an issue that had been around for a long time in one form or another had recently come to the surface and become quite intolerable. She talked about needing to address it and wanted to process a bit.

We talked and talked and eventually came around to the Centre. She said that this need to address the issue was definitely related to work somehow. She expressed bewilderment at how working at the Centre could have such an impact on her personal life.

"I know," I said. "It happened to me, too. You're hittin' the wall!"

The remarkable thing about this ordinary story is that when it comes time to give a name to this colleague, I could choose one of six names. They experienced the same phenomenon to lesser and greater degrees. This is not a wild coincidence. What I call "hitting the wall" was some kind of collision between professional and personal lives. People who came to the Centre and embraced its philosophy had to adjust the way they saw difficult kids in order to adjust the way they worked with them. If you manage to shift your vision or perspective in one area of your life, it will shift throughout. None of us realized the magnitude and impact of that shift until we began to see the impact on our personal lives.

Perhaps as we learned to feel comfortable with conflict, as we learned how to communicate more effectively, as we learned to problem-solve, as we learned to face issues head on, and then, as we saw that these things all had positive outcomes, perhaps we let go of some fears and allowed those new ideas to follow us home.

I remember one friend in particular who hit the wall around his relationship with his father. This was a well-balanced individual: loving relationship with his partner, clear career goals, smart, open ... you get the picture. With him, the process looked to me to create the fewest ripples. We talked about his relationship with his dad a few times. He agonized over it a little, but soon decided to talk to his dad and start making changes. I remember the morning he came to work and told me about that breakthrough conversation with his father. I remember thinking that he had handled that assimilation of professional philosophy and personal habits the best of any of us. It appeared minor to me, so I was surprised but happy to learn that he felt his time at the Centre to be a life-changing experience.

It seemed to cost different people different amounts of time, energy, and pain to get through that wall. Some people made major life changes. Others changed over time, and when they started taking that new person home every night it stirred up stagnant waters. Sometimes that just creates stinky water, but usually, if you don't like the smell, it leads to change.

There were occasionally people who came to work at the Centre who didn't stay long. I remember one teaching assistant who was very skilled but always seemed distant from the kids. I felt as if she was never happy at work. It seemed to be "just work" and nothing more. One day as we supervised the kids together, she started talking about the philosophy of the Centre and how she didn't agree. She believed that punishment was an important part of dealing with kids with behaviour problems. She was not with us long and I always wondered if her inability to explore another way of looking at difficult kids was really a strong professional belief or a fear of change. Sometimes the wall is just too scary a place to go.

For me, the process was about revelation. I am a bit thick at times when it comes to self-awareness. When I began working at the Centre, it was like picking flowers. I would see some interaction between staff and student, witness some skill or methodology being used and want to have it. I'd pick that flower for myself. But every time I picked one, I got more than I bargained for. It came up roots and all - I got the source and life of that skill or method, and then what could I do but take it home and plant it?

When my job forced me to be a better listener, I went home and planted that skill and nurtured it and it developed. Imagine the impact on all your relationships of that one skill alone.

When my job made me stretch my heart wider and wider with compassion, I took that big heart home. When it made me practise patience, I took that flower home - one I had not done a good job of growing at home in the past. When I learned to be calm during crisis and conflict, I took that home. As I got better at accepting responsibility for my mistakes, I took that home. As I learned to be gentler with myself and take responsibility for my own feelings of self-worth, I took that home. Everything I learned, every gift I received in my professional life, eventually became part of me.

We who have experienced hitting the wall have often talked about it, trying to understand it. I'm not sure I have explained my thoughts clearly enough here. I'm not sure that I fully understand the phenomenon myself. I just know that if you are working with others and helping them make changes in their lives, you better grab the handrail, honey - it's going to be a bumpy ride.

Chapter 10

If You Get Frustrated Take a Break

Why I am a dishwasher this year

I looked up from my desk just in time to see the pencil before it nailed me between the eyes. The student who had decided to share it with me was swearing a blue streak and stomping toward the Quiet Room. Our eyes met (mine freshly uncrossed), and he yelled at me, "I know. I know. If you get frustrated, take a fuckin' break!"

Although, ideally, we wanted kids taking breaks before they started throwing things, it was comforting to know he was attempting to follow our informal motto. Kids heard the "take a break" admonition in every context: if the game in gym was getting intense and someone's competitiveness was getting the better of him, we encouraged him to take a break on his own initiative. When someone was getting annoying to be with during lunch break play time, go play with someone else. If long division was just more than you could handle at the moment, do some different math, or maybe some science. If talking about what happened at your last school was too intense, take a time-out and go for a walk.

We tried to make sure that any kid with a low threshold for frustration (most of them) knew how to take a break. If you didn't set it up with them ahead of time and let them know where they could and couldn't go, etc., it was possible to end up with kids who hit their limit and either blew up, or shut down. Or, as in the case of one rather eccentric young man, they may decide to take a break, walk across town, and demand a meeting with the superintendent of schools.

Lots of kids just needed to be able to get up and move around when they felt a bit antsy. For them, asking to go to the washroom or to get a drink of water was usually enough of a break for them to refocus themselves (especially since getting a drink entailed going to the kitchen where there were inevitably kids from the other class working - a nice little exchange of unpleasantries is always a good way to break up a dull morning).

Some kids were habitual pencil sharpeners. I had one obsessive-compulsive kid who had to sharpen something when he needed a break, so I left a bucket of pencil crayons by the sharpener for him. Other kids had little jobs within the classroom that they could use as breaks: tidying the bookshelf, cleaning the blackboard, or whatever.

For those with hyperactivity problems, there were more involved plans. The many pets at the Centre were good for this. There were always a couple of fish tanks and several kids had a standing invitation to come by any time and see if the fish had been fed yet.

Then there were the breaks the adults decided were necessary. For students who were not yet able to recognize their own signs and call a time-out, the adults might assist. Probably the one I used the most was photocopying. Either I would ask a TA to copy something and suggest they take Sparky with them to help, or I would take Sparky myself and leave the group with the TA. This was a good long walk, a chance to chat, a chance to breathe, a chance to wiggle. Usually a student returning from the photocopier was all ready to resume work.

Occasionally, a very specific plan was needed. One boy and I had worked out a deal with the director that allowed the boy to deliver important messages from my desk to the desk of the director. They said urgent things like, "Hi Bob. Are you curling tonight?" The student knew they were nonsense - he also knew they were to give him a walk and a stretch, and if necessary, a chance to talk to Bob if he felt that was what he needed.

Kids who had the potential to be explosive, had their own plans in place as well. They knew where they were allowed to go if they felt that they were "losing it." There was the Quiet Room, the office, the kitchen, the couch, the meeting room, the back door and a walk around the building, the swings. The kids needed to know they had some space. Some of them needed to find their own spot with no suggestions from us or they would continue to run or hide everywhere. They created their own safe places. As a result, when certain kids stormed out of my class, I knew to look under the stairs, or between the doors, or behind the couch, or under the study carrel in the kitchen. (I also learned the hard way, not to go into those safe places uninvited!)

It was also okay to take a day off. If someone had an extraordinarily bad week and was losing control again on Thursday, it was acceptable for student, parents, and staff to agree to a day off on Friday and a fresh start on Monday.

So, what did I learn as I encouraged kids to give themselves breaks? Not a darn thing for several years. A bit slow on the uptake, I continued to work harder and harder as I grew softer and more flexible in my expectations of others, kids first and eventually, colleagues. While I tried to help kids open their minds to all kinds of possibilities for themselves, I ignored my own daydreams. While I preached the gospel of "You can do whatever you want with your life," I failed to see what I wanted to do with mine. Very slowly, I began to feel restless in my job. I had a hard time understanding this restlessness as I knew that I worked in a great place, worked with and for great people, and would probably never be in such a rich learning environment again. Yet, I was restless.

I took a leave of absence from my job, hoping some distance would allow me the perspective I needed to decide what should come next in my life, both personally and professionally. I went away on a retreat with that focus in mind and returned with the knowledge that the change I craved was about more than my career.

Today, I find myself living on a beautiful island, enjoying my life at a peaceful pace, and healing. I was surprised to find out just how tired I was. I sit here some days and the faces of students drift through my mind and I feel sad because I so often felt sad for them when I was with them. I couldn't fully feel all those things then; it would have been paralyzing to really think and feel about kids living in desperate and depressing situations with no apparent solutions. At the time, I think I limited my feelings in some way so that I could do my job effectively.

Working with people in any capacity is challenging work. I found working with students to be rewarding, yet the cumulative effect was draining. That could just be my over-identifying with kids; I'm not sure. I do know people who have worked with difficult kids for many years and remain effective, energetic, and enthusiastic. We are all different, and for me, the seven-year cycle proved to be right on target.

I still don't know if this break is all that I was seeking. Perhaps I will return to the classroom once I have written down and sorted through what I need to. I don't know. I do know that I needed to listen to my heart telling me it was time to go. Perhaps I should have gone sooner. But as I washed dishes this summer, I thought a lot about what I experienced and learned in the last seven years and my appreciation for my time at the Centre has grown tremendously. And I have finally fully absorbed my own lesson - it is an absolute necessity to take a break if you're feeling frustrated.

Every kid I worked with over the years has a tiny piece of my heart with them. They may not have clear memories of our time together, they may not even remember who I am, but they carry a bit of me, indelibly printed on their spirit for better or for worse. And inside of me, I carry a piece of each and every one of them - their incredible courage, their resiliency, their humour, their love, their strength, their spirit, their hope.

When I left the Centre, I felt that I might have given away a bit too much to the kids - my heart felt a bit small and fragile. After several months of rest, reflection, writing, crying the tears I did not allow myself at the time, I feel restored, and I think about all those little pieces of my heart walking around out there somewhere, and my heart feels huge.

Chapter 11

Thank you

At the end of one dishwashing day at the retreat centre where I work, I sat in the hot tub and relaxed. Another woman was there, enjoying a beautiful day and a beautiful view of the ocean. She introduced herself as Margie, and we began to chat. We got onto the topic of what I used to do before I moved here, and she was very interested in hearing about the RSC. She shared with me that she had experienced some difficulty as a child and as a teenager, and that she had memories of many "helping adults" in her life. She said that she didn't remember any names but she could see many of their faces and she felt they had made a difference in her life. We talked a bit more, and then she said that there were likely kids out there who remembered my face and would like a chance to say thank you.

She looked at me and said, "For all those people in my life who I never got a chance to thank, and from all the kids you worked with, I will say thank you to you. Thank you for making a difference."

She told me it was a powerful moment for her. I couldn't adequately express how it felt for me because I was overwhelmed. It was a huge moment of closure for me - a thank-you I didn't even know that I needed, coming from a stranger in a hot tub!

And so my final word to you is the same one - thank you. Thank you for hanging in there with kids when you don't feel like it. Thanks for caring when no one else will. Thanks for being generous enough to share your energy, compassion, and heart with so many little people who will never say thank you - to you. But maybe they are out there somewhere, sitting in a hot tub, thinking back, remembering your face and feeling grateful.

By the way, I later learned that the former "at-risk" youth in the hot tub that day was internationally renowned dancer and Order of Canada recipient Margie Gillis.

References

Long, N. J. , Wood, M. M., & Fecser, F.A (2001). Life space crisis intervention: Talking with students in conflict (2nd ed.). Austin, TX: pro ed.